My French Life

VICKI ARCHER   photographs by Carla Coulson

LANTERN
an imprint of
PENGUIN BOOKS

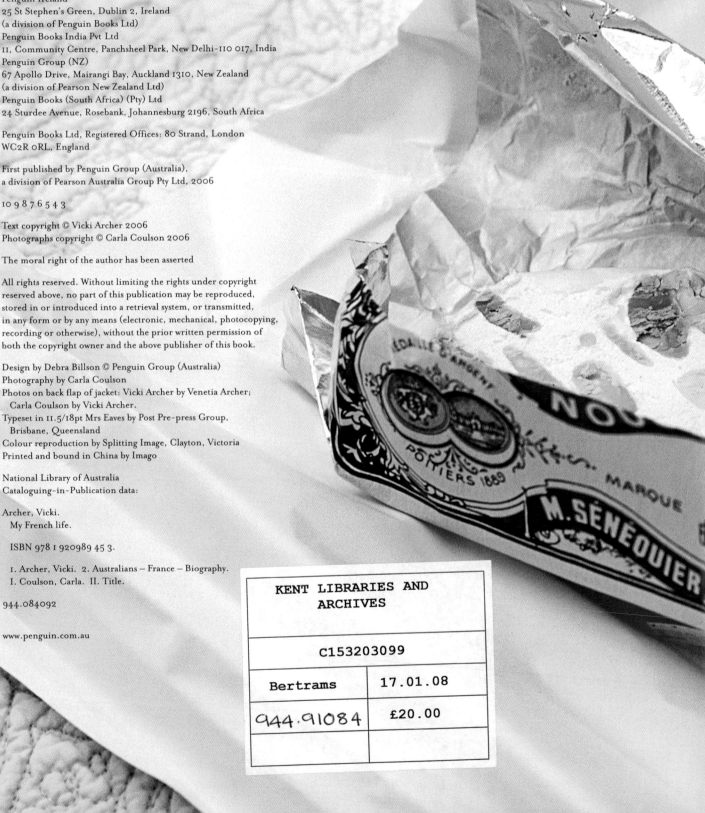

LANTERN

Published by the Penguin Group
Penguin Group (Australia)
250 Camberwell Road, Camberwell, Victoria 3124, Australia
(a division of Pearson Australia Group Pty Ltd)
Penguin Group (USA) Inc.
375 Hudson Street, New York, New York 10014, USA
Penguin Group (Canada)
90 Eglinton Avenue East, Suite 700, Toronto, ON M4P 2Y3, Canada
(a division of Pearson Penguin Canada Inc.)
Penguin Books Ltd
80 Strand, London WC2R 0RL, England
Penguin Ireland
25 St Stephen's Green, Dublin 2, Ireland
(a division of Penguin Books Ltd)
Penguin Books India Pvt Ltd
11, Community Centre, Panchsheel Park, New Delhi-110 017, India
Penguin Group (NZ)
67 Apollo Drive, Mairangi Bay, Auckland 1310, New Zealand
(a division of Pearson New Zealand Ltd)
Penguin Books (South Africa) (Pty) Ltd
24 Sturdee Avenue, Rosebank, Johannesburg 2196, South Africa

Penguin Books Ltd, Registered Offices: 80 Strand, London
WC2R 0RL, England

First published by Penguin Group (Australia),
a division of Pearson Australia Group Pty Ltd, 2006

10 9 8 7 6 5 4 3

Design by Debra Billson © Penguin Group (Australia)
Photography by Carla Coulson
Photos on back flap of jacket: Vicki Archer by Venetia Archer;
    Carla Coulson by Vicki Archer.
Typeset in 11.5/18pt Mrs Eaves by Post Pre-press Group,
    Brisbane, Queensland
Colour reproduction by Splitting Image, Clayton, Victoria
Printed and bound in China by Imago

National Library of Australia
Cataloguing-in-Publication data:

Archer, Vicki.
    My French life.

    ISBN 978 1 920989 45 3.

    1. Archer, Vicki. 2. Australians – France – Biography.
    I. Coulson, Carla. II. Title.

944.084092

www.penguin.com.au

to Suzanne

contents

ANCIENNE VOIE
AURÉLIA

50

Foudre
LOVE AT FIRST SIGHT

WHEN I AM ASKED the question, 'Where do you live?' I can only respond that there is no single answer. The truth is I feel I have three lives. I live a split life between where I was born and raised, where is feasible for my family and where my heart truly lies.

It all started so simply. I love to travel, I married someone who loves to travel and we had three children who were made to travel. My husband David and I had both 'been around the world' as children with our families – not an enormous amount by today's standards, but enough to want more as adults. We met and married in our twenties and have been travelling ever since. But it was travel for business or pleasure; changing our lives was not the intention, until September 1999 when we bought a property in Saint-Rémy-de-Provence, in south-western France. At this time we were living very happily in Sydney and had no thoughts of moving away permanently.

Together with our children – Emily, then fourteen, Venetia, eleven, and Paddy, ten – we fell in love with Mas de Bérard, a Provençal *mas* (farmhouse) sitting in the middle of 50 acres. We did not think about the reasonableness of owning a property on the other side of the world, nor did we consider at that time relocating in any real sense; our home was in Sydney with our friends and family. There was no planned objective or large-scale reflection to alter our lives. I describe it as *le coup de foudre* or love at first sight, because I cannot explain with any real logic why it happened. It was without doubt one of our most impractical moments as a couple.

I like to think it was meant to be. We were renting a house outside the village of Eygalières, ten minutes by car from Saint-Rémy-de-Provence, enjoying our holidays and

Plane trees line the roads of Saint-Rémy and in the summer months provide shade and relief from the searing heat of Provence.

contemplating the idea of owning a foreign property. Mornings and afternoons were filled with adventure and discoveries. Little by little the lure and appeal of this life became entrenched; the language came rather too slowly but the physical attraction was immediate. I had become infatuated with France some years earlier and David had long favoured France as a destination. We were drawn to this region for the beauty and peaceful ambience more than anything else.

Although we were taken with the idea of having a home in France, I am convinced we both thought it would be more a question of looking, talking and going through the motions; we would cure our interest and leave France with our dreams intact and our lives unaltered. Contemplation is a dangerous game. Looking became wanting, wanting became buying, and buying changed everything.

That day as we negotiated the turn into the driveway and made our way past the line of ancient plane trees and through the apple and pear orchards tunnelled in rich green coolness, and then over the canal glistening in the late September sun, we caught a glimpse of the Alpilles mountain chain, and I knew we were in serious trouble.

The farmhouse in view was not in line with the one in my imagination: what stood before us was derelict and in total disrepair. My excitement never faltered for a moment — these were mere hurdles to be jumped. My son, Paddy, whispered, 'This is it, Mum. We've found it.' My heart was hammering in my chest, tears filled my eyes, my ability to speak vanished and the momentous truth shook me like nothing before. If you believe there can be a moment in time when everything in your life changes, then for me, this moment had arrived.

We bought those 50 abandoned acres on the outskirts of Saint-Rémy-de-Provence. Thirty minutes from the centre of Avignon, forty minutes from Aix-en-Provence, fifty minutes from France's second-largest coastal city of Marseille and twenty-four hours by plane from Australia. Geographical location was vital to make international connections. We could fly into Paris and take the fast train to Avignon or arrive in Nice and drive to Mas de Bérard within two hours. Marseille Provence International Airport meant London Heathrow was

That day as we negotiated the turn into the driveway and caught a glimpse of the Alpilles mountain chain, I knew we were in serious trouble.

Gérard can turn his hand to any practical matter, however large or small.

only two hours away. We tried every alternative, but in February 2000 we gave in to the permanent jet lag and moved to London.

We anguished deeply over the move but hoped an international life would be an advantage for the children. We were confident that they were secure in their Australianness and would flourish in a new home. There was no question of moving in to Mas de Bérard, because the property was uninhabitable and would take years to complete, but both practically and emotionally we needed to be closer. Paris seemed too difficult given the children's ages, stage of schooling and lack of French language skills. Saint-Rémy-de-Provence was too remote. They needed to further their learning in an education system similar to that of Australia. In London my husband could continue his business life, we could educate our children and I could physically oversee the restoration of the farmhouse and the planting of the olives with a relatively easy commute.

I had never imagined myself as an olive farmer — I was a city girl, not the proprietor of an olive farm in the French countryside.

The nature of our terrain determined the planting of 20 acres with four mixed varieties of olives. The land in front of the farmhouse is dry and stony, a natural environment for olive trees. They thrive in the arid climate and high temperatures of Provence. Olives harvested and pressed for oil are more profitable on a long-term basis than the labour-intensive, back-breaking work required to produce apples and pears. When I first saw Mas de Bérard it was the plane-tree-lined driveway, the winding canal, the Alpilles Mountains and the stone farmhouse that were the heart-breakers. Now I view things rather differently. I have become an olive farmer. I nurture and fret over the olives like children and unthinkingly take for granted the 300-year-old plane trees.

As the scale of what we had undertaken emerged and the fog of enthusiasm lifted, it became clear that we needed permanent help to oversee the farm. A part-time *propriétaire*, however passionate or committed, was not enough. Our manager, Gérard, and his wife,

I have become an olive farmer. I nurture the olives like children and unthinkingly take for granted the 300-year-old plane trees.

*Running up the stairs at Mas de Bérard;
I remember climbing the steep ladders to
look up into the roof and stepping over
the gaps in the floor.*

Christiane, came to Mas de Bérard in November 2000. The land had to be cleared, the irrigation installed and the small olive trees planted and staked by hand. All this Gérard managed and supervised. Months later it was the demolition of the older parts of the building and the organisation and stockpiling of material that would occupy his time. His responsibilities changed as the months passed and the undertakings grew. Gérard can turn his hand to any practical matter, however large or small. He always had great faith and trust that together we would reinvigorate Mas de Bérard — now we shake our heads in disbelief and wonder how it was ever possible. The house is restored and breathing again, the garden is prospering, and the olive trees are tall and bearing fruit.

Six years on, this new life is complicated. What happens when raw instinct and unusual circumstance take the place of the well thought-out and certain? Our lives changed with one simple decision; everything I had taken for granted and known throughout my adult life transformed. My future and the future of my family became foreign. Our database of knowledge and inherent familiarity was no longer any use. A new existence emerged to replace the old.

I now divide my year between France and England, with several visits to Australia thrown in. My children spend most of their holidays at Mas de Bérard but would regard themselves equally at home in London. David is wherever we are and manages to work in all three places. We consider ourselves very much Australian yet accept that the majority of our time is spent out of the country. Our friendships have grown, not diminished. We have new friends in England and France, and longstanding friends who are very happy to visit and be a part of our novel life. The wonderful thing about living in another country or two is that the experiences keep multiplying. Our French language skills have certainly improved. Emily, Venetia and Paddy are more competent than David or me, having had the benefit of early study and exposure.

I am happy for the moment to share my time, knowing that Mas de Bérard is only a short journey away. My enthusiasm for being there never fades and every visit feels like the first. My heart truly lies in France for some inexplicable reason. I am devoted to our farm and captivated by a love of all things French. I have become comfortable with this split life and accustomed to the surprises and challenges it offers.

Somehow it works. ❖

le mas

THE FARMHOUSE

$\mathcal{S}$AINT-RÉMY-DE-PROVENCE sits on the north-western border of Les Alpilles, the 'little Alps'. These limestone mountains run in a ragged formation for 24 kilometres between the Rhône and the Durance rivers. Although the size of a small town — with 9500 permanent inhabitants — I have only ever heard Saint-Rémy affectionately referred to as 'the village'.

I love this village for so many reasons. I never tire of looking at the many historic fountains or wandering through the alleyways and secluded squares. The massive plane trees bordering the circumference of the village throw shade in summer and twinkle with lights at Christmas. Come rain, hail or shine the fresh produce market is held every Wednesday morning. Narrow cobbled streets wind inwards towards the *hôtel de ville* (town hall) and are home to small boutiques specialising in olive oils, wines, chocolates, biscuits, jams, candles or decorative wares. Tearooms, brasseries, *boulangeries*, *pâtisseries* and restaurants make these streets so individual. This is a village full of life and personality.

Saint-Rémy has been the home of some of history's best known figures. It was the birthplace of the sixteenth-century astrologer and physician Nostradamus. Vincent Van Gogh spent the last year of his life at the Clinique Saint-Paul-de-Mausole on the outskirts of the village. In 1889 he was admitted to this psychiatric asylum overlooking olive trees, wheat fields and irises. Inspired by the landscape, he painted some of his most famous works here, including *Irises*, *Starry Night* and *Wheat fields with Cypresses*. The views from the window of the room he lived in remain remarkably unchanged to this day.

Just south of the village are the two monuments known as *Les Antiques*: a mausoleum from 30 BC and an arch from 10 BC, built to celebrate Caesar's conquest of the Greeks and

The streets of
Saint-Rémy-de-Provence,
by day and by night.

the Gauls. These impressive gateways to Saint-Rémy-de-Provence are some of the best-known classical sites in France and mark the entry to the ancient Greek–Roman city of Glanum, unearthed by archaeologists at the beginning of the twentieth century.

IT IS SPRINGTIME and at our property, Mas de Bérard, the fruit trees are ablaze with delicate powder-puff blossoms; full and white, they shower like confetti in the breeze. The farmhouse faces south towards the sun, lean and simple against a backdrop of physical beauty. The garden is about to burst forth after the long winter, and the sound of birdsong is sharp. The Alpilles are almost turquoise today and they reflect and bounce their colour all over the land.

The stone on the side of the Ancienne Voie Aurélia discreetly marks the entrance to the *mas*. As you turn in, a dirt road winds through fields of olive trees. Five years old now, our plantings of this venerable species are beginning to take form and mark their presence. Like small children, our olives require nurture, love and constant supervision.

Mas de Bérard, dating back 400 years, is encircled by manicured gardens and sits in the middle of apple and pear orchards and olive groves. Built of local limestone ranging in colour from almost chalky white to rich cream, the farmhouse runs across the length of the garden. Small and large stones blend easily to create thick, imposing walls, making the house impervious to all weather conditions. The many windows and doors are protected from the penetrating Provençal sun by dove-coloured wooden shutters. The original terracotta roof is weathered, with highlights here and there of the rich colour it once was. It is edged with traditional scalloped tiles, three rows deep, allowing the heavy rains of the south to fall away in sheets.

The entrance to the house is through a stone archway and vaulted porch that leads to an outdoor courtyard, which is paved and patterned with local river stones and bordered with slabs of limestone. Classic pencil pines frame the space on all four sides and white roses cling to the walls of the house. On the left-hand side three wide steps lead to the wooden front door. The wood bears the patina of age and the waxed surface is smooth to the touch, preserved over the years by many loving hands.

Mas de Bérard, dating back 400 years, is encircled by manicured gardens and sits in the middle of apple and pear orchards and olive groves.

A terrace running the length of the house forms the focal point of our home. Each room downstairs opens onto this external living space and has uninterrupted views of the grounds and mountains beyond. The terrace is interrupted halfway by an iron-forged *treille* (arbour), the typical Provençal style of awning used to provide protection from the summer sun. Its frame is covered with purple wisteria and fruiting grapevine that tangle and weave above iron tables and chairs that live underneath all year long.

In front of the terrace, the spacious lawn is divided by a *chemin d'eau* (waterway). This path of water flows from an ornamental pond down towards a stone basin. Van Gogh-coloured irises border both sides of the waterway, and olive trees either side run parallel.

On one side of the *chemin d'eau* it is possible to walk through a covered wooden tunnel that spills over with roses of the palest pink, and to continue further past lines of pomegranate trees, their knotted trunks and chartreuse foliage directing the eye toward the apple orchard. In Spring, these rows of cascading white blossoms mark the end of the garden. Looking back towards the house a fountain, anchored against the southern wall, breaks the large expanse of stone. More scented roses seek the sun as they clamber up towards the master bedroom.

On the other side of the *chemin d'eau* is what we call 'the park'. This is home to the more established trees: chestnut, persimmon and cherry trees keep company with two magnificent pines, their fine needles and great cones carpeting the undergrowth. Thick bay hedges separate the park from the rest of the garden, and a statue of the Virgin Mary in her own grotto stands guard over these elders.

The sound of the running water is cooling and tranquil. Charlie and Nellie, our two dogs, stretch out languidly in the sunshine. Charlie, a Bernese Mountain Dog, is two years old with long dark hair, white facial markings and a playful disposition. Nellie is a short-haired blonde Mastiff with looks only a mother could love; she is a superb guard dog, frightening in size but devoted in nature.

Beyond the lawn, the orchard and the park, lavender beds clipped and full of promise give way to fields of shimmering olives and the limestone crags of the Alpilles.

Six years ago this was not the picture.

The discovery and purchase of this property has been a journey of unimaginable twists and turns. I never really grasped the enormity or the difficulty of the task. I leapt headfirst into the unknown.

The fruit farm had long since lost any real semblance of life. As markets changed over time and fruit farming as a way of life declined, most of the 50 acres had been abandoned. The original farmhouse was without any modern services, and access to the majority of the house was impossible. Over the centuries, renovations and additions had been made to the house and accompanying barn. Sections had been sealed up and left derelict, sadly neglected and long past their use-by date. Every square inch was uninhabitable.

To allow us to inspect the buildings a huge extension ladder was propped against the rough unrendered walls. Step after step I climbed through dust and darkness, searching for some idea of the room sizes and the overall layout. The area in front of the house harboured a variety of stone outbuildings accommodating all sorts of agricultural debris and farm equipment. The coming and going of cars and trucks over the years had ruined any remnant of garden close to the house. The promised view of the Alpilles was masked by this ancient mess.

Nothing could deter me, nothing would change my mind, it was too late: I had already seen the plane-tree driveway, the orchards and the flowing water of the *chemin d'eau*. The oaks, chestnuts and towering pines only strengthened my resolve. Our own Virgin Mary in a grotto in the park and a commemorative headstone to Count Bérard in the orchard were temptations too strong to resist. The prospect of a traditional stone farmhouse (albeit in a tortured state) facing the Alpilles clinched the deal. It was love at first sight.

It is springtime and at our property, Mas de Bérard, the fruit trees are ablaze with delicate powder-puff blossoms; full and white, they shower like confetti in the breeze.

Instead of sensibly climbing back in the car that first day and asking Valérie, our real estate agent, to show us her next property, I became more and more smitten. Meeting Valérie the week before in a neighbouring village, Eygalières, was one of those lucky chances. Her perfect grasp of English, generous personality and extensive local knowledge paved the way for us so many times in the following weeks.

Talking long into the night, David and I impetuously decided to follow our hearts, not our heads.

Meeting with a local architect was the first step. We needed to know if it were at all within the realm of possibility to restore this farmhouse. Hugues Bosc was filled with an excitement and enthusiasm for Mas de Bérard that matched my own. A talented man with impeccable taste and natural style, his confidence was inspirational and his vision wide. He understood with great depth and feeling what was required for this project. Within days we had negotiated and agreed with the owner, engaged a lawyer and signed a contract. Mas de Bérard was ours.

Completing the purchase, drawing plans and submitting them to the local council took six months. Restoring and rebuilding the farmhouse took almost three years.

The start was difficult. The language came to me slowly. All I had was a very basic level of schoolgirl French, and there was no time to enrol at language school. I needed immediate skills to communicate. Questions were mounting at an alarming rate. Stonemasons, plumbers, electricians, plasterers and carpenters all needed answers.

Learning a language happens in stages, and the first breakthrough is a limited understanding. Somehow the words began to make sense; I could not respond, yet I had a vague comprehension of what had been said. There were advantages to learning in Provence: the speed is slow and melodious and the conversations repetitive. If I did not grasp the idea initially, I persevered because the same words would be repeated over and over. Language is for socialising and enjoyment; it was important for me to understand these customs. A conversation would never begin without some form of preamble about the day and a little history of the project. There was always more than one way to attack any task and they all had merit and required comment. Discussions grew and developed, and time was never of the essence.

DE CORA AU CULTE DU SOLE

thko

er JEWELERS EXTRAORDINARY

Venetia, Paddy, Vicki, David
and Emily. Summer 2005.

Speaking French during the evening was out of the question in those early days. By the time the sun had set, so had my limited linguistic skills. The ringing of the telephone produced dread and mild panic, because I find speaking and understanding over the telephone much more difficult than face-to-face conversation — there is no way to read the body language or apologise with a little smile or shrug. Colloquial terms and fast-talking do nothing for my confidence or comprehension. To this day I am slightly nervous whenever I answer the phone at the *mas*.

Little by little the words built up and I managed to speak. I was encouraged by an extremely kind French friend who explained to me that the sound of someone trying to speak another language with a foreign accent is charming and rather quaint. Whether or not it is true, it was the break I needed. I stopped mumbling and blushing, and decided to forget about sounding French and concentrate on speaking French.

The French language is emotive. The verbs are strong and definite. The nouns are masculine or feminine. I could never understand why the farm would be feminine yet the farmhouse masculine; the pear and apple trees masculine yet the fruit feminine. Why are there so many words to describe a chicken? How can one French word explain so much? *La chaleur* (warmth) can describe the temperature of a summer's day or be an equally sufficient explanation of and excuse for a marital tiff.

Some days the words fly like a familiar song and other days they seem lost or buried deep within me. These are the joys and the challenges of a new language — like a pair of old boots, sometimes they pinch and squeeze beyond belief and sometimes they fit like a second skin.

Looking back, the picture today is so different in many ways but so much the same in others. The original attractions remain but the attachments are stronger. Tears of joy fill my eyes when I arrive and tears of sadness fill my eyes when I leave. Friends who saw the farm in the early days have only now admitted their amazement at the scale and magnitude of the project. The teams of people who worked on the house are content and proud of their craftsmanship. I cannot deny there were days when the degree of difficulty flaunted with my resolve and tested my patience, nor would I say it was a project for the faint-hearted, but with unflagging support from David and the children, I found this great confidence and passion to create our home in a new country. ✢

les artis

*T*OWARDS THE END of the second century BC the Romans pushed their empire from Italy into Provence. They constructed stone roads across the country, revolutionised water supply with aqueducts and brought classical architecture to the region. The Ancienne Voie Aurélia connected Rome to Provence and provided the link between their expanding territories. This was my new playground and source of inspiration.

Mas de Bérard was built of limestone quarried from the same local hillsides; water flowed through stone channels from the same underground sources; and the Ancienne Voie Aurélia, a Roman highway, is now our postal address.

The restoration was tackled in sections. The plan was to unify the original farmhouse with the adjacent barn and create a suitable living space. Together with our architect, Hugues Bosc, we decided to convert the barn into a kitchen and sitting room, with the master bedroom above. The farmhouse would become the dining room and guest bedroom downstairs, while above Emily, Venetia and Paddy would have their rooms. The connection between the two would be made from the kitchen into the dining room. This plan would give us a very open area downstairs with plenty of room upstairs for the bedrooms. Two staircases were required to access the top floor of this long L-shaped building. Monsieur Bosc assembled a team of craftsmen who began to plan the steps forward.

The first undertaking was a massive demolition and clean-up. There had been many additions over the years, both to the barn and around the *mas*, and we needed to rediscover the original dwellings to finalise the design. One of our fields was cleared and designated the *stockage* (storage facility). The outbuildings obscuring the main house were taken apart stone by stone, and the terracotta roof tiles were removed — individual pieces of both were numbered and stored for future use. Broken-down farm machinery lay alongside immense columns and metres of antiquated stone drainpipe; nothing was eliminated or deemed unworthy of revival. This 2-acre field was like a gigantic waiting room.

Each Tuesday morning at nine o'clock Monsieur Bosc and his assistant, Jennie Laplaisse, met with the stonemason, Monsieur David, and his team on-site. These *reunions des chantier* (site meetings) were memorable moments. Together we pored over hand-drawn plans, making decisions and discussing the merits of every option.

The painter's or carpenter's opinion carried equal weight with that of the electrician or plumber, regardless of whose area of expertise we were debating. Monsieur Bosc would sketch his ideas on scraps of paper for me when language became a barrier.

The site foreman, Guy, would stand back and listen intently, rarely speaking or taking notes. He knew it was his responsibility to turn creative chat into physical reality. Under his direction the water from the source now arrives in the house, using gravity in much the same way as the Romans did. The slope of the land provides the fall and the water is held in an underground cistern. The terrace and garden drainage system is a complex labyrinth and combines time-honoured methods with engineering genius. The foundations of the *mas* are solid and the roof resistant to the mistral, the icy wind that blows from the Massif Central in the north and accelerates through the Rhône Valley over to the north-west coast of the Mediterranean Sea. Blowing for days or even weeks at high speeds, this mistral (or 'master' as the Provençals call it) is fierce and causes the temperature to drop rapidly. Farmhouses in Provence were designed to be sheltered from this wind and insulated to retain their heat. Outside, the lines of cypress trees were planted as a barrier from the force of the mistral.

Jennie would shadow Monsieur Bosc, making endless notes. No detail eluded her and no dilemma was unsolvable. All the discussions, drawings and observations would then be neatly organised into note form and distributed. These weekly bulletins are a

Hugues Bosc, architect

Monsieur Mauron, plumber

Site foreman Guy, and
Monsieur David, stonemason

Monsieur Lançon, carpenter

Architect Jennie Laplaisse
and Monsieur Lançon

Monsieur Piak, tiler

Winter sunlight illuminates a corner of the sitting room. Long, lazy afternoons stretch into late evenings in front of the blazing log fire.

running commentary and truthful record. I loved to watch the artisans' rapt attention as Monsieur Bosc, known as *le chef* (meaning 'boss'), proffered suggestions. Each trade had its own *chef* in a well-rehearsed routine. '*Chef! Chef!*' could be heard all over the site, but there was never any doubt that Monsieur Bosc was the ultimate *chef*.

We had *rendez-vous* in the pouring rain and finger-numbing cold, in the searing 40-degree heat and 120-kilometre-per-hour winds. We anguished over large and small decisions. We agreed to disagree and we laughed often.

At one o'clock each day everybody stopped: labourers, stonemasons, electricians, plumbers, carpenters and painters had to eat. The Bunsen burners were cranked up and mouth-watering smells filled the air. The workers sitting in small groups reminded me of a schoolyard at lunchtime. Improvising, they made tables and chairs from the site materials, opened their picnics and uncorked the red wine. Fast food never seemed to make it here. After gorging on fat sun-ripened figs, some of the men would sleep for an hour in the shade. In the hotter months they rested in the middle of the day and worked in the cool of the evening; I would regularly see men labouring well past eight o'clock at night.

We often ate at the Bistro des Alpilles, a firm favourite of Monsieur Bosc, five minutes away by car, in the village of Saint-Rémy-de-Provence. We would sit at his regular table and order the house special: *gigot* (shoulder of lamb) spit-roasted over a wood fire, with huge helpings of creamy potato. Washed down with glasses of house red, it was an ideal end to the morning. After such intense concentration and decision-making, food and wine had never been so satisfying.

The stone walls of Mas de Bérard were dismantled rock by rock and found their way to pyramid-shaped stockpiles of large and small stones all over the site. A stonemason named Faysel selected each stone as he reconstructed the walls. Every day he would blissfully enthuse about the joys of Provence.

'*Bonjour, Faysel, comment ça va?*' I would ask him. With a broad smile that seemed to light up the site he would reply in English, 'I am wonderful – the sun is shining and we are in Provence.' Pleased with himself and his ability to deliver this line in English, he would inevitably break into song. Concentrating on one section at a time, Faysel determined the

Shoes kicked off at the end of the night. Waxed terracotta tiles carpet my bedroom.

size and shape necessary to fill the crumbling holes. Once he had made his selection he would use a small chisel to delicately chip away and shape the stone for the best fit. For two years he restored the walls in this way. He had an eye for perfection and a passion for his trade. The resulting stonework is testimony to his skill.

The traditional terracotta floor tiles were severely cracked. The stone floors were broken and patched in parts with concrete. The clay colours varied from the softest peach and yellow to intense oranges and vibrant reds. A *tommette* (hexagonal tile) in pale rose now carpets most of downstairs while upstairs butter-coloured squares have been laid on the diagonal.

Each hand-crafted tile is different. The size and shape varies, the colours lighten and darken, there are ridges and bumps in texture yet they blend together to create a warm palette.

The sitting room is paved with worn limestone slabs purchased before we had even completed the sale of the property; they lay idle for two years before they felt the touch of human feet.

Diak fashioned these floors, tile by tile, stone after stone. They were packed in huge wooden crates and carried by forklift from the *stockage*; a human chain would then unload and stack them inside wherever Diak was working. Together he and Monsieur Bosc, heads bent, would place patterns and decide which to reject and which to keep. As for the outside walls, each terracotta tile and limestone slab was individually selected. Diak laid them one by one on a bed of sand. A length of string tied to a wooden stick was his measure, and his talent provided the rest.

Vaults and niches were under the theatrical direction of Patric. With a deadeye he formed and shaped the ceilings or shelves using rolls of chicken wire and then applied layers of plaster, smoothing each out in record time before it set. He was a ghostly vision as he worked covered in a fine layer of white powder.

Bottom left: A faded English rose print in oyster linen upholsters the painted bed in Emily's room.

The local forger, Monsieur Aeillo, seemed to know what I wanted before I knew myself. He would nod vigorously over and over, repeating that he understood my request. Working alone in his atelier nearby, he would weld and file his handiwork until he was satisfied. Days later, sections of awnings, balconies or doors would arrive exactly as ordered.

I cannot remember the number of hours spent experimenting with Monsieur Gonzalez to find exactly the right shade and texture for the interior walls. Balanced precariously on simple ladders, his trowel laden with a blend of umber tints and plaster, he applied colour to the walls with a sweeping movement and a singular rhythm.

These craftsmen are living artisans and are, for the most part, native to Provence. Their techniques vary little from those of their fathers and grandfathers. Joy and pride in their workmanship distinguishes them. Such individuals left their stamp on Mas de Bérard — their signatures are the stones in the walls, the patterns on the floors, the balustrades of the stairs and the curves of the vaulted ceilings.

As the walls grew and the rooms took shape my adventures to furnish the *mas* began. I searched in villages I never knew existed and travelled to towns I had only read about. I encountered remarkable characters who were passionate about their fields of expertise.

On the edge of the small village of Flayosc, near the town of Draguignan, lives an antique dealer of some reputation. Welcoming me to Château du Deffends, she introduced herself as Madame Jacqueline Soulard. An elderly woman with a cropped grey shock of hair and the figure of a teenager, she was immaculately dressed from top to toe. Her home, her showrooms and her storerooms were filled with furniture and decorative pieces for sale. Mesmerising in her knowledge and formidable in her charm and persuasion, Mme Soulard is a French Mr Fix-it.

I happened to admire the exquisite *passementerie* (trimmings) on the remnants of a bed, and with the wave of her hand and a couple of finger snaps she had her able assistant, Jean-Marie,

MY FRENCH LIFE *les artisans*

This most fragile and delicate reminder of the past was brought back to life.

assemble it in no time. It was too short and had been water-damaged over the years. To my eyes it seemed unworkable. To her, nothing was impossible. Mme Soulard knew of only one artisan who could painstakingly unstitch the intricate *passementerie* and replace it piece by piece on a newly restored and upholstered framework. She made phone calls, produced swatches of fabric and extracted dates. It would take some time, but I drove away with the promise of an extraordinary bed for our master bedroom.

Months later Mme Soulard arrived at Mas de Bérard to present her creation. Jean-Marie assembled and installed the bed under her watchful eye. Patiently and willingly following her every directive, he positioned, lifted, filled and drilled until she was satisfied. This most fragile and delicate reminder of the past was brought back to life.

My hunt continued in the city of Nîmes. Behind the wide boulevards, the fine architecture of *Les Arènes* (the amphitheatre) and the preserved temple *Maison Carrée* (square house), Nîmes is a maze of small winding streets. Tempted by a display of simple chandeliers, I entered a tiny antique shop in the hope of finding some lighting for the *mas*. The gentleman owner sensed my keen interest and helpfully invited me to inspect his other storeroom. After locking his shop we walked, twisting and turning through narrow back streets until we reached a stone archway, where he unlocked a pair of wooden doors with an oversized iron key. The doors shuddered and creaked as he pushed them open. My curiosity was mounting, but by now I was comfortable with the unexpected and always thrilled by the French sense of drama. Pitch black until he flicked on the light switch, it was an Aladdin's cave filled with treasure. Needless to say, I found the lights.

In France I quickly learned that it is the things that are hidden behind closed doors that are the most remarkable. Not everything is as it seems.

While Mas de Bérard was still in the planning stages, Monsieur Bosc was eager to

select the front door. I thought it somewhat premature. I had no real comprehension of the different way restoration worked in this part of the world. New openings were cut to accommodate old doors not new doors made to fit old openings. Connecting the barn to the farmhouse meant a new entrance, and without a door the stonemasons could not determine the size of the opening needed in the walls.

Behind the village of Saint-Rémy, as I headed towards the old town of Avignon, I nearly missed the sharp right turn signposted 'Portes Anciennes'. I followed a narrow dirt road seemingly to nowhere, bordered on either side by green wheat fields stretching towards the horizon.

Inside Portes Anciennes thousands of wooden doors were stacked alongside ornate panelling and original window frames. There were doors belonging to local farmhouses, to châteaux of the Loire, to bastides near Aix-en-Provence and to Parisian apartments, from the very ornate to the more modest.

Walking up and down the aisles, Monsieur Bosc would digitally photograph our potential options. The choice was overwhelming. In his elegant, unassuming way he would quietly say, '*Pas mal, pas mal.*' I was baffled: normally our tastes coincided, yet he seemed to find these doors unattractive prospects. Literally translated, *pas mal* means 'not bad', which I took to mean tolerable. Colloquially, however, it is actually an expression of positive approval, almost exuberance. Eventually I understood his quiet words and we managed to choose the pair of oak doors for our entrance.

Plumes and pearls, silks and satins – this tapestry hangs in the guest bedroom downstairs.

We envisaged that the limestone fireplace in the *salle de séjour* (sitting room) would throw an enormous heat in winter and become the focal point of the house. The sitting room is generous in size but simple in style, and the fireplace requirements were the same. It would need to stand more than an average man's height if it was to look in proportion, and the lintel would need to be almost 1 metre deep.

I visited L'Atelier 13 at least once a month in my quest for the perfect *cheminée* (fireplace). Fireplaces, fountains, staircases and stone flooring were exhibited behind the village of Eyragues in L'Atelier 13's outdoor showroom. Once reconstructed, each piece would be numbered, and when sold it would be consigned to a stockpile to await delivery. A fine powder hung like a mist over the showroom and I would return home covered in this stone dust. The owner, Jean-François, spent his days on the forklift manoeuvring, reconstructing and dismantling pieces. Strewn and slouchy slabs of limestone would take shape and become living objects with hearts and souls. In one of these piles I found our fireplace. With precision Jean-François loaded and positioned the bars, balanced the slabs and supported the lintel. Our hearth was home and our home was on course.

In April 2002 we moved into the first completed section of Mas de Bérard: the barn and a small part of the connected farmhouse. We had an operational kitchen, a living room, two bedrooms and a bathroom. It was an impractical decision but one we wanted to make; our anxiety over things unfinished was replaced by an eagerness to be settled. Many of our personal belongings had been in storage since our move from Sydney to London, and we were impatient to unpack and arrange them. By this stage of the restoration I had stayed in every local hotel for my weekly commutes and was keen to have my own bed on-site, despite the many times I would be obliged to move it.

By December the following year the *mas* and the terrace in front were complete, the swimming pool was finished and the garden around the house was taking shape.

Mas de Bérard will probably never be finished; I like to think of it as more of a work in progress. ✣

In France I quickly learned that it is the things that are hidden behind closed doors that are the most remarkable.

les Femm

es

THE WOMEN

*L*E BON MARCHÉ, on the Left Bank, is one of the oldest and most beautiful department stores in Paris. It has been a Parisian institution since the 1890s.

I remember taking Emily, Venetia and Paddy to see the window displays at Christmas time in 1995. We had been holidaying outside the Mediterranean seaside village of Saint-Tropez and were commencing our trip back to Australia with a visit to Paris. My children, then aged ten, seven and six years respectively, rugged up against the unfamiliar cold, watched the animated puppets for what seemed like hours. Each scene was a tale of wonder that seemed equally to enchant the adults. In front of the glass, tiny viewing platforms had been built so that *les enfants* (the children) would have an unobstructed view. With a blanket of snow on the ground and the smell of roasting chestnuts infusing the evening air, I enjoyed the spectacle, thinking how strange and out-of-this-world it felt to be there.

Ten years later it is December, not quite as cold, but the windows are still enticing and small children are happily gathered. My cherished memories are swirling around me as I make my way into the store.

The cosmetics and perfume area is a well-designed oasis of calm. A consultant at one of the counters is tall with an auburn mane of hair and the *à la mode française* (in the French fashion) 1-inch fringe. Her translucent skin is glowing and her eyes are emphasised by some artfully applied grey shadowing. The shape of her mouth is definite and coloured with a burnt-red shade of lipstick. She is of an age that I can identify with: not a novice with line-free adolescent skin and equal lack of interest. This woman not only looks fabulous but she inspires confidence. There is nothing rushed or pushy about her.

Witnessing the visible transformation of others by her practised hand pushes me

Engrossed in her work, this woman enjoys a quiet cigarette on a rainy afternoon in Paris.

over the line: I too want to experience this skilful artistry. I want those sweeping brushes and soft patting movements to contour my face, the steady hand and eye for colour to enhance my lips and cheeks. She talks, I listen. Never stretch, only pat. She dabs, I pout.

I see that for a French woman, less is more. She explains that natural and simple only highlight beauty. Why cover life with an impenetrable mask? The lips are the most important, the mouth the focal point – they must be visible and strong. The eyes need to be outlined with reflective shades, not weighed down and closed. I feel confident armed with a new regime for the future: lips, lips and more lips.

Leaving Le Bon Marché on this chilly evening, I wander towards the Boulevard Saint-Germain. Ahead, two women and a small girl make their way towards the cafe Les Deux Magots in the heart of Saint-Germain-des-Prés. As early as the 1920s this legendary area was a centre for students, writers and artists living on the Left Bank. As these three take their seats outside, opposite the famous Church of Saint-Germain-des-Prés, a classic Parisian scene is set.

A picture of style, one of the women is wearing a wool overcoat the colour of ripe cherries. A large collar frames her pretty face and the bodice is nipped tightly around her waist.

Secured in the centre with large circular buttons, this bias-cut coat flares to just below the knee. The feminine shape emphasises her silhouette and the brightness of the colour warms the winter evening. Peeking out from underneath a cloche felt hat, her large doe-like eyes are clear and her dark hair is sleek and shiny. An expression of pleasure and contentment illuminates this woman's face. Pouring a soft drink for the girl, she glances up at her companion and seems to recognise the very same sentiments reflected in her eyes. They are sharing one of those rare moments of childhood innocence. Their precious little girl is deeply content, without a care in the world.

Peeking out from underneath a cloche felt hat, her large doe-like eyes are clear and her dark hair is sleek and shiny.

Valérie is always smiling. Here she sits in the garden at Mas de Bérard last Christmas.

I have always wondered where that certain *je ne sais quoi*, a sort of quiet confidence, exuded by French women comes from. My French friend Valérie shrugged at my question and told me she does not know the answer.

Valérie is thirty-six years old, born and bred in Paris, and now lives in the south of France with her husband and two daughters. I first met her when I visited the real estate agency where she worked in the small village of Eygalières in 1999. We have been firm friends since that day. To Valérie, friendship is about time spent together. Earlier this year she came to London for a girls' catch-up and a few days of shopping. As her departure time approached I brought a cup of coffee into the bedroom where she was trying to pack her too-small suitcase. She said thank you but she would come and sit at the table and drink hers with me. I suggested that we lacked the time to sit and chat if she was to make her train. She looked confused, and at first I thought it was a language misunderstanding. Not at all.

In Valérie's world, if there is no time to enjoy a coffee together, what is the point of drinking it alone? Coffee is about companionship, not caffeine. As a friend Valérie is generous, loyal and trustworthy. I have lost count of the number of times she has helped me navigate my way through French custom and bureaucracy to solve a problem. She is never too busy and does not know the meaning of the word 'no'. I understand why as a child she was nicknamed *ma petite Cendrillon*, 'my little Cinderella'.

Valérie does have that certain French 'something'. She has an enviable personal style and looks that could stop traffic. Her dark hair is forever changing style and is always well cut. With only five minutes to get ready she would never leave home without *les lèvres* (the lips): liner, colour and gloss, in that order. With somewhere special to go, she will gear up her eye make-up a notch, but generally she is a natural beauty. Her posture, from many years of dancing, is definitely an advantage: she never slumps; she always glides, even when rushing. Valerie explained to me the secret of her styling success: *marier les choses ensemble* (the way things are put together); *il n'y a pas de hasard* (it is never by accident). In her opinion there is no such thing as thrown together or luck. Her advice is to begin with what you are in no doubt of and what makes you happy. Take the time to feel secure in your choices and the rest will follow.

Begin with what you are in no doubt of and what makes you happy. Take the time to feel secure in your choices and the rest will follow.

MY FRENCH LIFE *les femmes*

french women know that the time
spent in the preparation of beauty
is not to be undervalued.

Shopping with Valérie, I learned that the most important thing for her was to wear what pleased her. She did not dress to fit in with fads or to impress girlfriends; Valérie selected what she genuinely loved. She wanted the latest but only if it flattered her. She chose by feel and texture. She searched out colours that suited her rather than those dictated by fashion. She saw what I would never have seen and had the self-assurance to put together combinations that worked.

For Valérie, her mystique, her *je ne sais quoi*, is confidence and contentment. There is no greater magnetism than a woman who is self-assured. This is the ultimate beauty secret and one that French women truly understand.

Every French town seems to recognise the importance of beauty, if the number of perfumeries, hairdressers, lingerie shops and pharmacies are an indication. However small the village or large the town, there is always an abundance of these stores.

A green-and-white cross is the symbol of the pharmacy all over France. For *les femmes*, this is a world of temptation. Special brands promise to stretch and smooth, colour and tweak. There are skin bleachers and wrinkle smoothers, fat busters and body creams — follow the directions and they guarantee a brand new you. Lotions to wax and polish, skin care and homeopathic wonders for the smoothest grease-and-oil change. There are medicines and prescriptions for every bug bite, allergy or infirmity known to humankind. The more old-fashioned pharmacies with their carved wooden shopfronts, gold lettering and large window displays are rapidly vanishing. The pharmacy on the Rue du Faubourg Saint-Honoré in Paris sells everything from hairbrushes and hairclips to hand mirrors and manicure sets. The assistants dress in white lab coats and dispense all manner of advice. It is long-established service where the customer counts.

There is a practice in French pharmacies and perfumeries of giving away a multitude of cosmetic samples with any purchase. Generous quantities of *échantillons* (samples), with advice on the application and benefits of each, is the norm not the exception. French women know that the time spent in the preparation of beauty is not to be undervalued.

Whenever Emily, Venetia and I are together, the pharmacy is one of our first stops. They love the unfamiliar brands, the stylish packaging and the variety. The presentation and wrapping are as important as the goods themselves in France. The girls collect a couple of the

There is no greater magnetism than a woman who is self-assured. This is the ultimate beauty secret and one that french women truly understand.

small *paniers* (baskets) sitting at the entrance and systematically search the aisles. Our visit to the pharmacy can last indefinitely; however long is never long enough for their liking. They never seem to have too much lip gloss or to tire of buying eyeliner and eye shadow; this mascara is so much better than their others, or so they tell me. The hair products, brushes and clips are essential and the bronzer is sensational. Although born in Australia, my daughters have adopted the same devotion as French girls to the pursuit of beauty.

Their bathroom at the *mas* smells heavenly, and their shelves and cupboards are stacked with all the girlie goodies. Much loved for its generous size and comfortable furnishings, it is more like a dressing room than a functional space. Their bath is an old-fashioned style, white enamel and freestanding on four legs, and it sits underneath the window with a view towards the Alpilles mountains. An antique gilt mirror, shaped like a sunburst, sits above their commode-style basin and a worn Aubusson tapestry chair sits in the corner. Scented candles and bath oils are arranged beside the tub on a tiered *étagère* (shelf). With their clothes strewn about in typical teenager disarray, it is their private female haven.

SEVERAL YEARS AGO female preparations of another kind consumed Mas de Bérard. Stéphanie, the daughter of our managers Gérard and Christiane, was to be married at the beginning of September. Fertilising, weeding and pruning suddenly ran to a marriage calendar not an agricultural one.

Traditionally in France a marriage is formalised in the local mayor's office, and the legalities are then followed by a church blessing. This wedding was to run over a weekend in Saint-Rémy-de-Provence. The bride was to leave for the church from the home of her parents, next door to Mas de Bérard.

Emily, Venetia, Paddy and I wanted to see Stéphanie dressed in her gown, wish her good luck and congratulate her parents before they left for the village. As we walked down the driveway I was surprised to see the bridegroom. The bridal cars, parked outside the house, were polished to a high shine and decorated front and back with lavish bouquets of apricot

Venetia

Although born in Australia, my daughters have adopted the same devotion as French girls to the pursuit of beauty.

roses. Imagining a problem, I thought how unlucky it was for the bride to see the groom on her wedding day before the ceremony. Reflecting on my own bridal butterflies, I presumed that marriage customs in France were similar to ours in Australia.

To my further surprise, not only were the bridegroom and his attendants there but his friends and relatives too. There were probably fifty people milling around outside the house dressed in formal wear.

I envisaged all sorts of last-minute romantic drama. Had they had a row the night before? Why was he there? Was it just a case of cold feet? Stephanie's brother welcomed us, shook our hands and suggested we stand in the shade to wait. More confused than ever, I discreetly asked him if there was something wrong. He looked at me with that blank expression I have come to know so well – the look that only the distance of a cultural divide can explain – and said, 'We are waiting.' Often when in 'French doubt' I say nothing, tilt my head slightly and nod agreement. I have invented my own mannerism to suggest that I understand. I have discovered that all will be revealed in good time if I am patient.

The children and I tried to hang back and assume as invisible a pose as possible. We had arrived direct from the swimming pool, with wet hair, barely covered and not looking our best. Conscious of not intruding, I had thought we would have five minutes with Stephanie, take a few photographs for her parents and leave. This was not to be; I was introduced to the waiting family and friends as *le patron*, a position of respect and importance in rural France quite unlike anywhere else. They were far too polite to remark on our dishevelled appearance.

Fifteen long, embarrassing minutes later the front door opened to allow the visiting hairdresser and make-up artist their exit. Excited little gasps escaped the crowd and I realised there would be no melodrama; it was routine for the bridegroom, family and friends to wait while the bride dressed. I have since gathered that it is French custom for the bride and bridegroom to leave her home together.

Stephanie appeared on the arm of her father and we all applauded. She had that wedding-day luminance as she turned gently towards him, kissed him on the cheek and told him she loved him. With tears in his eyes he squeezed her hands gently and bade her a silent farewell. He was about to share one of the women in his life. ✣

les sente

THE SCENTS

*T*HERE IS A DISTINCTIVE scent in the air. Tiny clumps of grey-green thyme mingle with bushes of sapphire-blue rosemary flowers to give off a heady fragrance. A light rain the previous night has enriched the colours, enhanced the perfume and energised the atmosphere. It is early February and the Alpilles mountains are blooming.

This time of year is normally ideal for walking: cool days with no risk of fire, views to take the breath away and pungent smells to stimulate the senses.

We have decided to climb up through a saddle in the Alpilles near Château Romanin and hike along the ridge line. Friends from London arrived at Mas de Bérard the night before, making us a group of nine. Bright and early the next morning everyone is dressed and ready for action. Walking boots and polar fleeces good enough for Everest are lined up in preparation for our hike. Backpacks are stashed with the essentials plus the not-so-essentials, and between us we have enough gear for a military operation.

We drive to the aerodrome at Romanin, 2 kilometres along the Ancienne Voie Aurélia towards Eygalières, where we leave the cars and make our way across the runway to the start of the walk. In true French style the direction for the *grande randonnée* (big walk or hike) is marked by two shocking pink slashes on the nearest tree trunk. These symbols, painted on rocks and trees, will guide the way. Inevitably we straggle along behind each other, finding our place and chatting away. David is our team leader, armed with a 'male' sense of direction and prior knowledge of the walk. Our second-in-command, Steve, is an experienced and capable hiker from way back. He thoughtfully follows behind to ensure the team concentrates on walking and not talking.

The walk starts easily as we meander along a stony path through overgrown bushes and inhale the blossom of the *garrigue* (scrubland). As we breathe deeply, the air almost startles our lungs; it bites with freshness. We climb in single file as the limestone path becomes steeper. The small packed stones give way to large shale-like chips, which slip and slide under our feet and make balancing difficult.

Leaving behind the near-vertical slope, we are filled with relief and much bravado as we reach the easier gradient, but not for long. We have conquered the sharp incline only to be slapped with an incredible gale, the mistral. This wind can howl for days on end. Provençals believe that it will always blow for an odd number of days, and my recollection is that this is true. According to local legend the mistral can cause depression, headaches and irritability — everything and anything can be blamed on the mistral. This adds a different dimension to what was meant to be an easy hike. We decide to forge ahead and brave the elements.

One after the other we hunker down low and head for the ridge line. This is not just a wind but a force of nature. Conversation ceases as the cracking gusts make hearing impossible. We are like Michelin men in our parkas, pumped up and propelled forward out of natural sync, trying to keep pace. To this madness we lose hats and anything else that is not securely held. Secretly I am regretting this foolishness; we have taken leave of our senses. Any self-respecting local would be tucked up inside warm and cosy on a day like today. But our little team is intrepid and we reach the summit.

Standing on this chain of mountains is like surfing the crest of a wave: frothing and foaming peaks lap one after the other into the diamond-clear distance.

The valley of Les Baux stretches out before us, and the snow-capped peaks of Mont Ventoux are within our grasp. We spot Mas de Bérard from our vantage point and are amazed at how far we have walked. Trying to stand upright in the 150-kilometre-per-hour wind on the edge of the ridge is a dare against the environment. Our smiling faces are hammered by the gusts. We keep moving; it is not the day to dally. The view might be flawless, but the wind is relentless. This mistral is a symphony in full swing.

David

On the grey and overcast days in London, I imagine Mas de Bérard: the scent of the iceberg roses, the lilac and lavender; the apple trees and their sweet-smelling blossoms...

Looking through to the dining room from the terrace in the early evening. The pewter plates sitting above the fireplace form part of a collection I found at Château du Peffends.

The descent is harder. Exposed, we must follow the ridge line to find our way down. Once on the path among the sparse vegetation, we are less protected than on the more precipitous slopes. A few of the girls run down, because it is easier than keeping in step with our dance partner, Monsieur Mistral.

After battling the mighty elements we reach the flats and relax. Our two-hour promenade has turned into a five-and-a-half-hour encounter. There is nothing like the feeling of wellbeing after a tiring day of outdoor adventure – exhilaration punctuated equally by moments of great calm and doses of high drama. We return triumphant.

Mas de Bérard has never looked so welcoming, the bath so enticing and the smells wafting from the kitchen so delectable. The aroma of Christiane's *bœuf en daube* (beef casserole), slow-cooked over three days, sends our senses into overdrive and makes the long trek worthwhile. Feeling like the walking wounded, we have worked up a well-deserved thirst and an enormous hunger.

The log fire warms our wind-chilled hands and feet as the red wine soothes our jangled nerves. Sitting around the table we relive every moment, telling tales, embellishing incidents and savouring the intense moments of the day. For once in France we have earned our lunch.

When I think back to that day it is the scents that are the triggers. I commit to memory the mistral, but when I inhale the perfume of wild thyme and rosemary I can see the girls, heads down in the *garrigue*, collecting their herbs to take home – a little piece of the Alpilles to linger in the city long after the French country holiday is over.

On the grey and overcast days in London, when the pace and the crowds are relentless, I imagine Mas de Bérard: the scent of the iceberg roses, the lilac and lavender; the apple trees and their sweet-smelling blossoms; the olive groves with their spicy tang after the rain. I close my eyes, picture the farm and count the days until I will be there. These familiar scents are the remedy, my antidote to the intensity of London life.

Lavender is the classic heroine of Provence, and it is impossible to usurp her position. Blooming in June, she lasts well through July and into August. In fragrant bursts she is the cologne of our summer.

Three shades of lilac flowers grow in profusion among the large bay hedges at Mas de Bérard. Lilac is almost wild in this part of the world and considered standard issue, but I cannot take for granted this delicate and tumbling bundle of purple happiness. I remember too well the days of paying dearly for a bunch, struggling to keep it alive just to enjoy the subtle fragrance for a day or two. Bay leaves in profusion have a softer and gentler bouquet than I remember from my dried-packet days in the city.

Verdant green fennel flowers and clumps of wild mint pop up in our fields between the rows of olive trees, signalling that spring is on the way. The piquancy of the fennel and the freshness of the mint combined with the smell of mown grass is a potent cocktail.

The smell of wood burning in our large stone hearth makes me think of laughing and talking all hours of the day and night. The lavender bundles and dried pine cones burn together with the logs and sweeten the air. But it is the small flickering candles scented with orange blossom and tuberose that really remind me I am home.

Kitchen aromas are in a league of their own. Slow-roasting ripe tomatoes fill the house with a scent like no other. The pungency of the garlic and parsley accompaniment seems to hang in the air and tease the tastebuds. Fruit thickening away for hours on *la cornue* (our traditional French oven) to make jam conjures up memories of my wiry husband up the ladder searching for the ripest figs or the juiciest plums. When I open a jar of blackberry jam I am reminded of my daughters and their friends picking the wild berries and returning with laden baskets and violet-stained hands. With the first waft of fruit blossoms on the wind my mind recalls our earliest fruit-picking adventures: gathering pears and apples, the stickiness on our

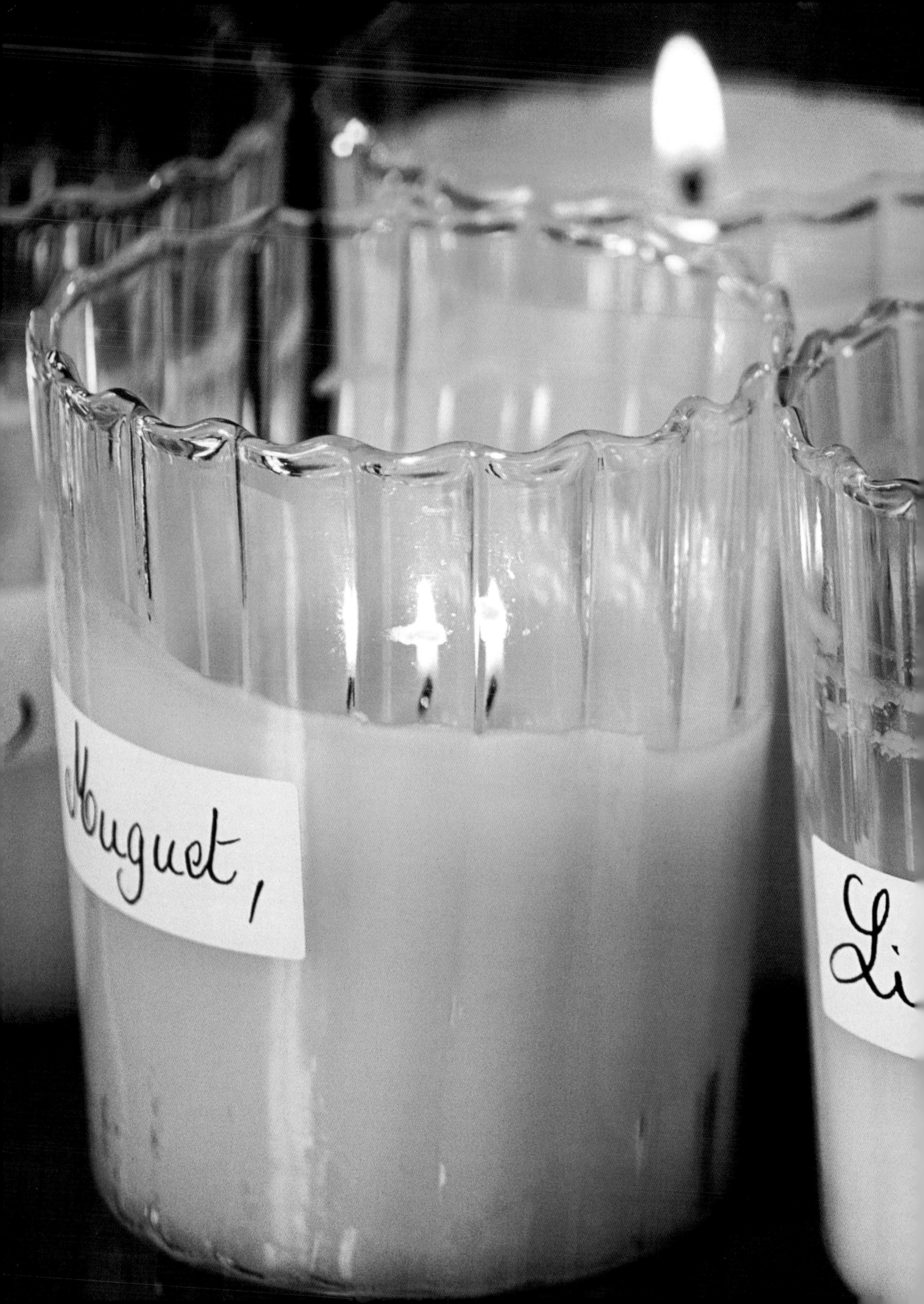
Muguet,

Blackberries that grow by the side of the canal, wild strawberries and local raspberries make the most luscious jams.

PATISSIER

hands and faces as we all raced to fill our baskets — somehow the scent of the blossoms, picking the fruit and baking the tarts all roll into one.

Each morning as I leave for the *boulangerie* I promise myself today is the day to avoid temptation. A block away and the smell of freshly baked bread is enough to weaken my resolve. Unsurprisingly my baguette order swells to include *croissant*, *brioche* and *pain au raisin* or *pain au chocolat*. A new recipe this year called the *garriguette* — a soft loaf topped with olive oil and *herbes de Provence* — bulks out our order, along with thick slabs of wood-fired pizza. When I hear Marie's Provençal accent imploring, '*Un petit goût*' (a tiny taste), and asking what else I would like *ensuite, ensuite* (next, next), I am lost.

Then there are the perfumes. French perfume has always had associations of allure and mystery, luxury and extravagance, style and originality. The most famous of these fragrances is still No 5, created personally by Mademoiselle Chanel in the 1920s. The mere mention of Chanel conjures images of Frenchness, glamour and beauty. The packaging, the classic black-topped bottle filled with silky pink body lotion or the square glass bottles of golden liquid, sealed with fine thread and rectangular stoppers — these have become symbols of true lavishness.

To create these subtle blends is a unique profession in the hands of a select few men and women, the 'noses' of the perfume industry. A passion for fragrance, natural talent and many years of strict apprenticeship are needed to become a great *nez* (nose). The creation of a perfume requires the knowledge of thousands of essences but the blending of few. The character of the perfume is determined by three elements: a key note, the scent that is instantly discernible and memorable; the core notes, which denote the overall nature of the fragrance; and the basic notes, which hold the essences together.

Choosing a personal fragrance should be an unforgettable experience. A scent is more than a few dabs on the wrist and a brief squirt behind

the ears; perfume is personal magic. It is a first impression and a lasting recollection, an invisible guide to personality, a key to individuality. It stamps your signature and leaves your calling card.

Fragrance creates lasting associations. I remember the scent of my first bottle of Arpège, a gift from my father so long ago. When I think of my wedding day, I recapture my walk down the aisle in a cloud of Joy. The mere hint of Des Lys or Rose Absolute reminds me of my daughters. Perfume is the last thing children smell when their mother kisses them goodnight. It is the one thing I never leave home without.

There is a ritual to buying perfume in France which is like no other. When I enter a *parfumerie* (perfumery) in Paris I enter a truly feminine world, a showcase for the sensuality and intimacy of fragrance. Essences of orange and lily, rose and violet, honeysuckle and jasmine, musk and amber create the mood. Packages of gold and silver, coloured ribbons and jewels, powders, potions and puffs give the feel of a personal boudoir.

The choice of a scent is a pleasure not to be rushed. A woman with an angelic face and classic gamine haircut offers her help. We discuss at length the latest editions and the more popular scents for the warmer weather. She is interested in my thoughts and proffers suggestions to tempt me. I am a single-fragrance kind of girl. I am truly committed and rarely unfaithful, but I am happy to be persuaded. Even when I play truant, it is never long before Gardenia Passion hauls me back. A harmless little flirtation with Fleurs d'Oranger or Le parfum de Therese only makes me appreciate her more. The assistant understands my loyalty and politely acquiesces to my past. In this *parfumerie* there is never a bombardment of fragrance without mutual consent. As she showers me with my long-term love I am coated in femininity.

A sense of smell is one of the wonders of life, and what better place to indulge in this miracle than France? ✤

SATURDAY MORNING   The doors to the Métro hiss with life as they open. Along the platform, up the stairs, through the turnstiles, Paris unfolds. It is early morning and the smell of freshly baked baguettes penetrates and wafts underground, lending an unusually delicious aroma to this public place. The sound of a busker bellowing his rendition of 'Hello Dolly' is amplified in these winding tunnels and floats toward the exit. Daily dramas are all around — undercover police disguised as street kids, couples enjoying a private moment before their day begins, or travellers busily counting stops and memorising Métro-line colours. Moving places and changing faces — this is a living documentary film running all day every day.

First stop: Palais Royal. Savouring the prospect of a few days alone in this irresistible city, I am already conscious that a weekend in Paris is never enough.

Café Le Nemours sits on the Place Colette, in the corner of a grand stone colonnade. Outside, chairs and tables face the square and imposing heaters give a warm blast to this otherwise chilly day. Inside, crystal chandeliers and matching wall lights topped with red silk shades are reflected in the mirrored walls. The centrepiece, a wood-panelled bar, is home to a selection of wines and liqueurs. Two large paintings framed in ornate gilt are hung at either end, lending perspective to this long, glamorous space. The atmosphere is sumptuous but not formidable.

Locals like to take their morning coffee at the bar on their way to work — a quick cup, a catch-up chat and a short glance at the daily news. Visitors prefer to choose a table, soak up the atmosphere and take their time analysing the passing parade. The spectacle of men and women, young and old, crossing this well-worn place in colourful coats and scarves is well worth the investment of time and a few extra euros.

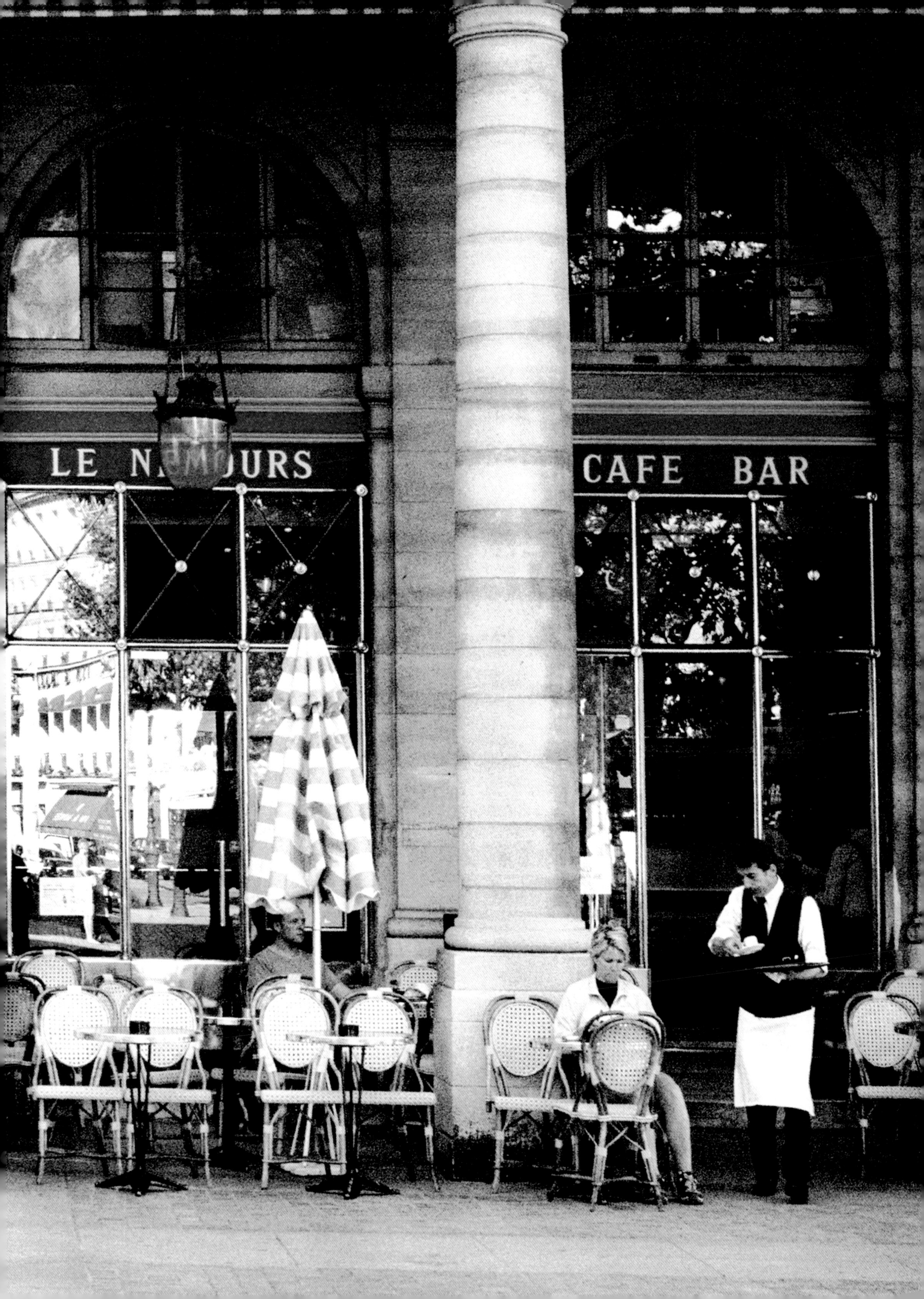
CAFE BAR

Seated outside are two eye-catching young women with their petite companions, a Chihuahua and a King Charles Spaniel. Perched high on their respective owner's knees, in the lap of designer luxury, these gorgeous creatures clearly want for nothing. As the two women become absorbed in their chat, the animals become restless. Wriggling and snapping, they somehow gain control of their leads, jump down and tear off into the distance without a backward glance, clicking and clacking over the cobbles as fast as their furry paws can carry them. The girls are hampered by indecision and 4-inch stilettos, so the ever-obliging waiter sets off after the dogs.

Of course this is a matter to be taken seriously — these dogs are in disgrace — but to see the long white apron, black pants, scalloped waistcoat and bow-tied 'penguin image' of our leggy attendant flying in pursuit of two pint-sized pets puts a smile on all our faces.

The three of them return to much applause as my coffee arrives: a double espresso, rich and strong, the first heart-starter of the day. I know I am in Paris.

Crossing the Place Colette and entering the gates to the Jardin du Palais Royal is a little like entering a past world. The gardens and the palace were built in the seventeenth century and served as the childhood home and later the hunting grounds of Louis XIV. By 1780 the palace was floundering under a mountain of debt, and arcades and shops were constructed on the site for commercial purposes.

Today exclusive boutiques line this space alongside grand restaurants and cafes. Daniel Buren's black-and-white candy-striped column installation in the centre of the court-yard provides a wonderful playground for children of all ages, and the silver mirror-ball fountains at the opposite end of the garden offer a quiet sanctuary for the less athletic. Simple but highly ordered, this is a space full of contrast and surprise, where classic meets the unpre-dictable head-on and lives happily ever after.

Retail spaces here are small, individual and very often unique. A music-box vendor,

Dominique at Didier Ludot.
Her twinkling eyes, calm manner
and full scarlet smile win me over.

located in the gardens for more than twenty years, sits alongside a shop dealing in old war medals and decorations. A specialist selling pipes and related
curiosities for the smoker trades beside one of the largest dealers in military
figurines.

Hair is coiffed at Trés Confidentiel behind white curtains and a veil
of secrecy. Only the name discreetly running across the shopfront alerts to the
style and glamour inside. Even the resident pup matches this salon's decor.

Didier Ludot has a series of boutiques specialising in vintage haute
couture. Loved by collectors the world over, the clothing of Chanel, Cour-
règes, Christian Dior, Balenciaga and Schiaparelli startles in museum-style
display. Irresistible vintage accessories and costume jewellery are housed in a
separate boutique. The third boutique – the one that entices me this particu-
lar morning – sells only one thing: the little black dress. Inside the boutique
I am welcomed by Dominique, in her own little black dress. Petite and fine-
boned, she has a sweet face framed with short dark hair marked by a single
blaze of white. Her twinkling eyes, calm manner and full scarlet smile win me
over. Within minutes I am in the dressing-room, desperate to step out of my
clothes and slip into grown-up elegance.

A spray of Fleurs d'Oranger with a hint of tuberose wafts out the
door of Les Salons du Palais Royal Shiseido. Created by Serge Lutens, this
fragrance is one of eighteen delicious *eaux des parfums* sold at this boutique.
Fleurs d'Oranger is one of those fragrances that can transport and change
a mood with a single dab; it can cause strangers to stop and pay the most
charming of compliments.

The Jardins du Palais Royal have a sense of seclusion; they feel like a
secret place of my own. They are relaxing yet stimulating, crowded yet solitary
and never the same in autumn, winter, spring or summer. Whether I come here
to stroll through the 8 acres of gardens and enjoy the symmetry of perfectly
placed lime trees, to admire the architecture and reflect on past history, to hop

Red geraniums tumble
from the windows at the
Hotel Plaza Athénée.

on and off the black-and-white columns like a child, or to fulfil an extravagant shopping fantasy — my weekend would not be complete without meandering around this much-loved garden.

A shot resounds; it is midday in the Jardins du Palais Royal. A small cannon installed in 1786 and fired every day signals it is time to move on.

As I cross over the Rue de Rivoli, intending to walk through the Jardin des Tuileries towards the Champs Élysées, I detour. Carved in marble and around 8 feet tall, a goddess of victory stands alone on the landing of the Daru staircase in the Musée du Louvre. A Greek statue dating from the Hellenistic Age, she was found scattered and broken on an island in the Aegean Sea in 1863. As I take the Denon entrance and head slowly through the galleries, she appears like a floating vision. The placement of *The Winged Victory of Samothrace* is starkly dramatic yet appears effortless. Framed in architectural beauty and powerful natural light, she provides the perfect place to pause in this huge, daunting museum. Her outstretched wings and rustling garments suggest for a moment that the chilly breezes are blowing strongly. A shiver escapes me, and for a split second I can imagine her serenading the victorious Greek vessels as they return home from battle. She sits so comfortably at the apex of these stairs, many miss her beauty and incredible presence in their rush to see her most famous rival, the *Mona Lisa*.

I leave the Louvre and race up the Champs Élysées. The day is slipping by all too quickly. In the blink of an eye I have passed some of the most historic and breathtaking sights of this city: the Place de la Concorde, the Luxor Obelisk and the Grand Palais.

These symbolise real grandeur in a very French way. Guilty for my neglect, I reflect on their magnificence and their unfailing ability to enthral — but it is lunchtime in Paris and I am running late to meet my friends Martin and Debbie.

Chez André on the Rue Marbeuf is one of those old familiar haunts that my whole family loves, and one I like to introduce to my friends. This classic brasserie sits in the area known as the Golden Triangle, the traditional heart of haute couture, between the Avenue

Daniel Buren's black-and-white candy-striped column installation in the centre of the courtyard provides a wonderful playground for children of all ages.

Enjoying her aperitif, this woman is oblivious to the sounds of the city in the seventh arrondissement.

des Champs Élysées, Avenue Montaigne and Avenue George V, in the eighth arrondissement. Martin and Debbie are waiting inside, so the three of us hustle our way to a table in the back of the restaurant. The atmosphere is alive with locals and visitors packed in and laughing, talking, eating and drinking. This is like a game of chess. The waiter, with a lifetime of practice, pulls out the table in one sweeping gesture. Standing by, we watch closely for our cue. He makes two moves sideways, one move backwards and a slip to the right. Now our turn: breathe in tightly, don't upset the china and glassware, avoid an up-close-and-personal encounter with the next table, and lunge for the chairs. The manoeuvre is complete and we are seated.

Brasserie eating is intimate and noisy. We sit on traditional plush velvet seats while dramatic lighting highlights the tightly packed, linen-covered tables. These are spaces full of colour and life. The decor is complete with large, elaborate mirrors.

All diners are equal in the brasserie; people-watching is a must for everyone. There are no blind spots, passers-by can be seen by all. Inside, daily menus suggest the catch of the day, the freshest vegetable of the season or the specialities of the house. Of course no self-respecting French diner would enter without having first consulted the board outside. Waiters and waitresses rush to and from their tables, only too happy to discuss the merits of one dish over another. Dressed formally in black and white, the waitresses particularly are reminiscent of a past era. Wearing dainty white aprons with thick frilly edges and a generously tied bow, these women make their way around the restaurant with an elegant swish.

The bread basket is replenished and the soft peach-coloured rosé poured; our anticipation of the roast chicken and chips is mounting. The noise level is resonating, there is a pleasant lack of mobile ring tones and everyone is engrossed. From time to time a slight tilt of the head and a quick scan by the eye suggests that the room is being worked. Nothing goes unnoticed or overlooked. Reflections in the mirrors, people passing by, entrances and exits — these are not ignored. Perhaps it is the light but flavoursome gravy, not too heavy and not too thick. Perhaps it is the crunchy golden *pommes frites* (chips) alongside the moist succulent chicken. Or is it perhaps the real pleasure of people-watching in a city that has made it a national pastime? This is one of my favourite Saturday lunches anywhere, anytime.

SATURDAY AFTERNOON   Winter sunshine and clear skies make this the perfect after-noon for a *promenade* (stroll). I am a cold-weather person, so November and December are the months I love in Paris — the temperature is cool and the atmosphere crisp. Outside, the buildings seem like one giant silhouette against the cobalt sky. Our plan is to walk towards the Avenue Montaigne, which runs all the way from the Champs Élysées to the River Seine, offering a commanding view of the Eiffel Tower nearer the river.

It is 3.30 p.m. and the Avenue is buzzing. Very grown-up shoppers with serious transport are lined up and down on either side. Cars with darkened windows are manned by uniformed drivers; merely looking at them seems indiscreet. Manicured canines on designer leads, glamorous women wrapped in thick fur coats and carrying Kelly bags in all sizes and colours are out in force today. These beautiful classics from Hermès claim their turf, never missing a beat alongside their more contemporary designer rivals. In this arrondissement, young and old still pay reverence to this chic French status symbol.

Martin, Debbie and I cross the Seine and walk along the river. The view is timeless: bridge after bridge after bridge. With the Eiffel Tower behind and Notre Dame ahead, this is

An old-fashioned winter scene in the Jardin des Tuileries: children sail their boats across the pond and onlookers relax on the chairs spread around the edge.

sightseeing at its very best. The Left Bank and Right Bank each has entirely different atmosphere, yet they are divided only by the narrow width of the river. It is possible to cross between these worlds in the space of five minutes, moving from glamour and opulence in one *quartier* to the more casual and creative in the other.

The Rue Bonaparte on the Left Bank is a narrow cobbled street leading to Saint-Germain-des-Prés. On the corner, Ladurée, originally founded in 1862 on the Rue Royale, has opened a *pâtisserie*, tearoom and chocolate shop. Pale grey walls are hung with miniatures and engravings, and the sumptuous navy-blue velvet chairs and banquettes prove very inviting. The low, round tables are set with Ladurée's distinctive mint-coloured porcelain. The menu offers sweet temptation after sweet temptation and a wide selection of Indian, Chinese and English teas. We are only too happy to sit, relieve our tired feet, revive with a cup of tea and sample the house speciality: the macaroon.

My first macaroon from Ladurée counts as one of my life's memorable taste sensations. Once bitten *not* twice shy. They were impossible to resist, a complete awakening and a greedy memory to laugh over. These delectable mouth-watering biscuits come in an assortment of sherbet colours and a variety of flavours. Making the initial choice is impossible, so I recommend an assorted box: there will be a sweet moment for everyone. Ladurée's macaroons are the perfect gift: perfect for the person impossible to buy for, perfect for the person you are longing to buy for.

After saying my goodbyes, I meander down the Rue de l'Université, which is crammed with all sorts of charming boutiques. I turn into the Rue du Bac, admire the interior-design shops and then follow the Rue de Grenelle from start to finish. The style of Left Bank chic is evident here: less predictable, more colourful and intrinsically unique.

Musée Rodin on the Rue de Varenne is so close that I have a little time to wander in the gardens and appreciate the backdrop of large-scale sculptures. Inside Hôtel Biron, home to the permanent collection, there is a group intently gazing at *The Kiss*. Their guide is pointing out the delicateness and sensitivity of Rodin, the carving of the hand and the intimate touch of the slightly lifted finger on the female's body. Even ten minutes in this beautiful museum is enough to restore my fading energy.

SATURDAY EVENING   Tonight I am staying in the area known as le Marais with my friend, photographer Carla Coulson. This fashionable *quartier*, the oldest on the Right Bank, lies between the Hôtel de Ville, the Place de la Bastille and the Place de la République. I have stayed with her many times in Paris over the past year as she photographs *My French Life*.

Carla's apartment is on the sixth floor. Residential streets in Paris are full of hidden surprises. A carved wooden door of immense proportions discreetly bearing the number means I have arrived. Knowing the six-digit door code allows me to cross the first threshold without a problem. The big wooden doors make a distinctive click and bounce open to reveal a massive stone courtyard. It is stark and austere, the evening darkness broken only by an overhead lantern. I walk toward a further pair of imposing iron gates; code again, click again, and the spring releases. A long stone passage, a double set of glass doors and I am ready for the ascent.

As I mount the steep, curving, tower-like stairs, three flights pass without too much difficulty. Reaching the fourth landing, my breathing is laboured, my overnight bag heavier and my pace a little slower. Arriving on the fifth floor, I decide a rest stop is definitely in order. The last part of the climb is a surprise: not a conventional staircase but a ladder. Balancing like this is for ballerinas. Each time I climb it I cannot help but wonder how Carla manages with all her photographic equipment, shopping bags and clutter of life. Stair-climbing in Parisian apartments must be the secret of French longevity. Many dainty steps later, my ascent is complete, the summit has been reached.

Entering the apartment, I am enthralled by the view over the rooftops of Paris to the luminous Colonne de Juillet on one side and to the dome of the Pantheon on the other. This is a view to climb for. Every second of this day has been hectic and I have set myself a frantic pace, but tiredness is a master I cannot ignore. We eat in.

SUNDAY MORNING   There is a market at the Place de la Bastille each weekend, and if you live in this *quartier* of Paris, it is the natural place to shop. Food markets are generally held in the morning, and are always better earlier rather than later.

Entering the apartment,
I am enthralled by the view
over the rooftops of Paris to the
luminous Colonne de Juillet on
one side and to the dome of the
Pantheon on the other.

Platters of oysters, mussels, prawns, lobsters and scallops are prepared outside. Seafood displayed on the pavements is part of the brasserie tradition.

The Place de la Bastille is a huge interchange, with the Colonne de Juillet as its impressive centrepiece. The Colonne de Juillet represents the victims of the Revolution and is crowned with the figure, 'Spirit of Liberty'. Last night, the view of this golden figure from Carla's apartment appeared anchored and angelic above the illuminated column; on a day like today she glistens and gleams in the winter sun.

The market is held on one side of this large square. To welcome us, a twenty-piece brass band is playing. Some couples are dancing. The idea that Carla can do her weekly shop to live music appeals to me. Somehow a foot-tapping beat outside in the sunshine quickens the heart and spices up the most mundane of tasks. Buying potatoes and onions has never seemed so much fun.

Meanwhile, the aisles between the stalls are already congested. The entire city seems to be trailing shopping caddies and stocking up for the week. In striking colours and with personality galore, these caddies are wheeled by young and old. Red, purple, yellow, green, patterned and plain, they are a definite must-have. A little like overnight bags in waterproof nylon or canvas, they effortlessly roll along. Capacity is generous, yet when empty they fold up to nothing. Mothers and tiny daughters walk side-by-side with matching colours but different sizes. Some men and women parade with elegant or more sombre designs, others manoeuvre a chosen check and the very brave trot out leopard and zebra prints. There are families with multiple caddies full to the brim and those with empty caddies ready to shop. The woven basket might reign supreme in the country, but the caddy has cachet in the city.

Packing the caddy is something of an art. The locals are expert: they reserve the space at the top for their most fragile produce; the baguettes poke out of the corner, tall and straight, like soldiers standing to attention.

Wheeling our new purple and red caddies, Carla and I walk down the first aisle. Every food imaginable is on display. Piled high, there are fruits and vegetables spilling over the tables, and glass cases full of meats and cheeses, with countless numbers of *saucisson* (sausages and salamis) hanging like thick roped necklaces above. Eggs are placed one on top of the other in the shape of pyramids. Fish (whole and in fillets), shellfish, oysters, scallops and

MY FRENCH LIFE *le week-end*

A favourite lamp found in the markets of Serpette and Paul Bert, Saint-Ouen, Paris.

crabs are stacked high on ice-filled trestle tables. It is impossible to resist these vendors and their compelling tales of freshness and quality.

By one o'clock the mood has changed. The packing-up has begun. The stalls look depleted and the crowds have vanished. Lunch beckons.

SUNDAY AFTERNOON   This afternoon Carla and I stroll around the antiques markets of Saint-Ouen. While these days the markets are no longer a well-kept secret, they are somewhere I continue to visit. Over the years I have found many of our family's sentimental belongings here: mirrors, beds, doorknobs, picture frames and embroidered linen sheets. The pleasure is in the search, and the finding provides lasting memories.

These flea markets are enormous, some of the largest in the world. Not the most scenic of destinations, they run over some fairly indifferent terrain, but the trek is worthwhile. Walking from the Métro station at Porte de Clignancourt is a navigational challenge. There are acres of fake-leather bags and jackets, African souvenirs, toys and Indian cashmere to be pushed past. The Rue Paul Bert is the main street and entry point for most of the antique shops and markets. Laneways are maze-like and seem to ramble forever. Cafes and restaurants are dotted among incredible furniture and endless French bric-a-brac.

The Vernaison Market on the right-hand side is home to 'Lili et Daniel'. I collect old cloth trimmings, and this shop is overflowing with them. Wide or narrow, in every shade, there are boards and boards of exquisite silk ribbons lining the side walls. I can't resist: I buy 3 metres of the palest pink and cream and 4 metres of chartreuse and purple. Delicately embroidered, they will enhance a cushion or wrap a Christmas gift. The back of the store spills over with tassels and braids and the doorway bulges with boxes of multi-coloured buttons.

Further down this street are the antique markets of Serpette and Paul Bert, my personal choice. With only an afternoon to spare, these are by far the easiest to explore. Wandering along these alleys, I am fascinated to see how the many dealers style their individual stands. They feel private and intimate, like entering a small salon, a library or a bedroom. All the dealers roam, chatting with their colleagues, speculating on the numbers of clients passing through and which nationalities they might be. They know who is looking and who is spending. As much as the vendors in the food markets love discussing their fresh produce, so too do the antique dealers enjoy talking about their wares. I love to hear the origins of a specific hoard and how they came upon it. Sometimes I am sure the story is questionable, but it takes nothing away from the tale and there is no obligation to buy.

One of the joys of French life is taking the time to talk about the small things; spending ten minutes or thirty discussing something of mutual interest and enjoyment with a complete stranger. The large mirror now hanging in our stairwell at Mas de Bérard was sitting angled against a dark wall at one of these stands several years ago. I made a general enquiry that started a long conversation about where I came from, where the dealer came from and ultimately where the mirror came from. Monsieur Papillon had been to a sale in northern France and bought the entire contents of one family's home; the older generation had passed away and the younger members of the family were ready to move on and begin their lives in the city. The mirror had hung in a small salon for over fifty years, so the hand-gilded frame and mercury glass were in near-perfect condition. We chatted at length and he showed me other pieces he had purchased at the same time. Eventually we agreed on a price over an espresso and a long reminiscence about Saint-Rémy-de-Provence. A search for wonderful pieces was his life's passion, and he was genuine in his enthusiasm. He was delighted to share his knowledge with someone of similar mind.

SUNDAY EVENING It is Sunday evening at the Gare de Lyon. I am taking the TGV fast train home, back to the peaceful life of the farm and the sunny skies of Provence. I feel like the country mouse leaving the big city behind. It has been exhilarating to sample all the wonders of the city and enjoy the different pace. A weekend in Paris is like a tablespoon of elixir: it should be taken full strength and on a regular basis.

As the train pulls into Avignon station, the doors open for their three-minute interlude and I scramble to gather all the spoils of my weekend before disembarking. Outside I breathe in deeply, taste the freshness in the air, see the brightness of the stars. David is standing on the platform waiting to collect me. I cannot wait to be home. ❖

A weekend in Paris is like a tablespoon of elixir: it should be taken full strength and on a regular basis.

er et

Dîner
LUNCH AND DINNER

*B*ON APPÉTIT: **TWO SIMPLE WORDS** in French; a single phrase that rings out loud and clear in restaurants, streets, beaches or any place between the hours of 1 and 3 p.m. It is customary and polite in France to wish 'happy eating' to all.

Tuesday morning meetings at Mas de Bèrard always finished with '*Bon appétit.*' The waiter who places your food on the table will say, '*Bon appétit.*' If you pass a friend or colleague in the street at lunchtime the conversation will end with '*Bon appétit.*' When you leave any shop, bank or office at one o'clock, the parting words will be '*Bon appétit.*'

In the south of France it is taken for granted that everybody will break for lunch and enjoy a proper meal. Business stops and appointments cease; the entire workforce comes to a halt. Decisions, from those of small consequence to those of the greatest magnitude, must resume after lunch, because there is nothing so important that it can interrupt eating and digestion.

Food is an integral part of French life, to be shared and savoured. Eating on the run is not an option. Fast-food outlets are scarce. Time is the key. It is vital to undertake the lengthy preparation and it is customary to appreciate the eating.

'*Coucou, Coucou,*' Christiane calls as she arrives back from the Wednesday morning market in Saint-Rémy-de-Provence. This sweet little country expression in place of *bonjour* is often used as a greeting for the second encounter of the day. Christiane has cooked in our kitchen for five years. She is a local woman, born and raised in the nearby town of Cavaillon. A true Provençal, with a melodious accent, she can feed ten or fifty without batting an eye. Entering the kitchen, she has two large baskets filled with the lettuce and berries for

Loulou from the village helps Christiane prepare a warm salad of goat's cheese in the kitchen at Mas de Bérard.

lunch, and carefully balanced on top is a tray of soft white cheeses. Each piece is hand-wrapped in white paper and placed snugly next to another in a woven straw platter. Christiane rarely ventures to the market, preferring the modern, less-crowded ease of the local supermarket. I, on the other hand, hardly ever miss Wednesday morning's chance to buy the season's finest. Under Christiane's command the kitchen responds lovingly and willingly. Her vinaigrette dressing, traditional tarts and tomatoes Provençale are renowned among our family and friends. One day I asked Christiane the secret to her cooking. The answer was simple: 'Take the time.' She never seems to mind spending the long minutes to hull the tiniest of wild berries or to finely slice the fragile *cèpes* (wild mushrooms). Taking two days to prepare her tomatoes or hours to roll pastry is the least she can do for a deserving meal. In her very calm way she responded to my question by telling me I am mostly in a rush, sometimes too busy and very often preoccupied with thoughts other than food to be a successful cook. It was not a criticism but a cultural observation.

It is early June and we are eating outside with Valérie, her husband Patric, and their daughters Manon and Tessie. The table is covered with a *Côté Sud* taupe-and-white cloth. These soft putty shades are the new feel of Provence, often replacing the brighter and more patterned blues, greens and yellows favoured in the past. The mocha-and-cream plates are alternately laid. A selection of water, wine and champagne glasses in shades of violet and pink are set in place. A pair of old patterned porcelain jugs, filled with slightly blown roses from the garden, decorate the centre.

The French are passionate about tableware — dressing the table is part of the whole dining ritual, as important as the food to be served — and I seem to have caught the bug.

Christiane has prepared one of our family's favourite menus. To begin, a delicious green-leaf salad with toasted walnuts, thinly sliced endive and her unbelievable vinaigrette. Next, a choice of fine pastry tarts — one filled with slow-roasted tomatoes, the other with

*Melt-in-the-mouth
Lavender ice-cream from
the teashop Charmeroy.*

caramelised shallots — which melt in the mouth and burst with southern flavour. A creamy Saint-Félicien cheese follows, to be eaten with the remaining light, crusty baguette. There is dessert if we dare. Who can resist scoops of lavender ice-cream and bowls of fresh berries? All this washed down with a delicious Château Romanin rosé from down the road.

WITH THE SUMMER TEMPERATURES soaring and resident teenage pressure rising, we head for the coast. There is nothing like the beach club to keep everyone happy. A reservation for the day entitles us to valet parking, sun beds, umbrellas and towels. Waiter service on the beach and sheltered restaurants mean that good food and wine are available all day. Pampelonne Beach, Saint-Tropez, is home to one of the best-known beach clubs, Club 55.

It is 14 July, Bastille Day. David and I arrive early with Emily and her friend Olivia, and make our way across the bamboo path to Club 55's section of beach. A bronzed and handsome — the main requirements on the job spec — beach boy sets up our beds, plants the signature umbrellas and lays out the towels. Each beach club is distinguishable by colour. Everything at Club 55 is pale blue.

The sand is already full of sunlovers. The water has that Mediterranean calm, and toddlers run in and out of the gently lapping waves. The fashion statement this year is the caftan. Made of sheer fabric, embroidered or jewelled, it is *the* attire for lunch. The most gorgeous women in skimpy bikinis, *shift du jour*, designer sunglasses and stilettos head to the restaurant at one o'clock. Men wear the customary Vilebrequin swimming shorts; the really smart have found the limited editions from the boutique in Saint-Tropez. This is the year of the Athens Olympics, so the *short du jour* pays homage to the Greek flag.

The restaurant is decorated with patriotic blue, white and red to mark the date. The tables are covered in flowered Provençal cloths, and the waiters, dressed from head to toe in white, seem to balance on air as they rush to and from the kitchen with steaming plates.

Huge woven baskets of raw vegetables — radishes, cucumbers, tomatoes, lettuce and carrots — are waiting on the table as we join our friends and sit down. Some of us order a fresh tomato, mint and crumbled goat's cheese salad with a mustard dressing; others choose the

The day is sapphire-blue, hot and dry, without a cloud in the sky.

mussels cooked with garlic and white wine. The salad has a distinct tang and the leftover dressing is perfect to be soaked up in the endless soft bread. The fresh catch of the day is sea bass, a firm favourite with our table. Barbecued whole over a charcoal fire, they are presented for inspection and then expertly de-boned before serving. A light pouring of olive oil, a squeeze of lemon juice and a smattering of sea salt for everyone; it tastes of summer days . . .

Further down the coast toward Monte Carlo sits the old fishing port of Saint-Jean-Cap-Ferrat. This waterside playground is overlooked by little shops and restaurants trading away the summer months. Villas and hotels cling to the steep hillsides, and the narrow winding roads are filled with cars playing chicken; Clios and Peugeots duel alongside Lamborghinis and Ferraris. It is the end of July and we are staying with our English friends Alan and Jane in a pretty pink house covered in bougainvillea and within walking distance of the port. They have six children ranging from eight to twenty years of age: Bertie, Jacob, Hermione, Leo, March and Noah.

The harbour's berths are locked down with speedboats, sailing yachts and fishing vessels. Moored out to sea are luxury liners – international passports to pleasure – with names such as *Enigma*, *Cover Drive*, *Arctic Princess* and *Octopus*.

A straggle of pink sails floats by; in single file a morning sailing class of small children grip their masts as they play follow-the-leader.

The day is sapphire-blue, hot and dry, without a cloud in the sky, and we have been speeding around the coastline by boat all morning with Alan and Jane. They have summered here for most of their lives and know much of the history in and around 'the Cap', but our gang of nine children is much more interested in bumping through the waves, sunbaking and the occasional quick plunge than taking in the sights.

Today it is the 'yellow' club for lunch. Accessible only by sea, this beach club in Cap d'Ail is built into a rocky part of the hillside and clings to the jagged coastline. We throw down the anchor and swim the short distance to the beach, Plage Mala. The tender has picked up our dry gear and already dropped it at the shore. A pathway of coconut matting from the water protects our feet from the large pebbles that make up this small cove. This trail leads to out-door showers and lines of yellow sun beds and umbrellas. Yet more good-looking boys lay out the towels. All the girls are smiling. Above the beach a series of suspended wooden platforms have been built over the rocks to form the restaurant. There are tables and chairs to eat at or sofas and umbrellas for relaxing. Ice-cold buckets hold champagne and soft drinks. We sit at a long table in the shade, Tahitian-style.

Every fixture and fitting in this beach club is grass-thatched or carved. Even the house Mojito tastes of the tropics; the concoction of rum, lime, mint and sugar hits just the right spot. Appetites screaming, the boys order hamburgers and chips; the girls are more adventurous with their *grandes assiettes du sud* or large mixed salads of spiced chicken with chilli and coriander. It seems that however small or isolated the beach, or however difficult the terrain, come one o'clock there will always be somewhere to enjoy good food.

AS THE SUN DROPS over Eygalières, one of the most beautiful villages near Saint-Rémy-de-Provence, men charge their glasses of cloudy alcohol and skilfully drop their *boules* onto the fine gravel surface of the local square. The metal balls clink together as *les vrais provençaux* (old-time Provençals) drink in synchronised accord; a lifetime of comfortable friendship meeting over a drink.

The apéritif *is both a drink and a time of day (six o'clock, give or take an hour). It is a reason to meet and a reason to quench the thirst.*

The Bar du Centre is warming up and bottles of Pastis 51 make their rounds. This aniseed liqueur from Marseille is a direct offspring of the notorious absinthe and is drunk with water and lots of ice; one part Pastis to five parts water. The number 51 refers to the year that Pernod first produced this blend. It is very much a man's drink, almost a Provençal ritual and a most definitive taste of the south. The villagers gather around the smoke-filled bar, the smell of Gitanes cigarettes strong, and gossip about the day.

Saint-Rémy-de-Provence

food is an integral part of french life, to be shared and savoured. Eating on the run is not an option.

*David relaxes around the dining-room table
with friends Bill and Adrienne after our
long hike in the Alpilles. Flickering candles,
glowing embers and delicious Hauvette wine
make a perfect end to the day.*

At home it is the catch-up part of the day, a time to meet on the terrace and chat. Rosé champagne served 'vodka cold' is our summer *apéritif*. Our accompaniments include black tapenade, plump green olives stuffed with goat's cheese and almonds from the Wednesday market, spicy sausage, roasted cashews and pistachios from Thursday's market trip to Maussane, and always the small savoury biscuits flavoured with wild fennel and olives from Le Petit Duc in the village.

IF TIME WELL SPENT eating is the moral of this tale, then the chef must be the hero of the story. French chefs learn their craft from a very early age – apprentices can start work as young as thirteen. In a Michelin-starred kitchen, a *stagiaire* (trainee) or *commis* (assistant) almost never cooks for the first year, sometimes spending more than twelve hours a day on menial preparation. Their tasks can be tedious and repetitive: learning the difference between good and bad quality, washing lettuces or peeling potatoes. Many of the most highly regarded chefs in France have begun their careers this way. In the late nineteenth century Georges-Auguste Escoffier developed a chain of command in the kitchen that is still widely used today. His principles were threefold: authority, responsibility and function. The *chef de cuisine* (head chef) sets the culinary standard of the kitchen and is assisted by a *sous chef* (deputy chef). The kitchen is then divided into specific production areas, each under the management of a *chef de partie*. Assisted by the many apprentices, each *chef de partie* will refer back to the *sous chef*, who strictly follows the principles and directions of the *chef de cuisine*.

The chef's tall white *toque de cuisinier* (chef's hat) varies in size depending on pecking order in the kitchen. The head chef may wear anything up to 12 inches high. The story goes that the extra height enables the *chef de cuisine* to be spotted quickly and easily in a crowded kitchen. A 'starred' kitchen must operate with military-style precision. Following orders and strategic planning are essential if the restaurant is to maintain its Michelin rating.

The *Michelin Guide* was first published in 1900 and was given free to motorists in France, offering suggestions for accommodation and food. In the 1920s, this little red guide introduced a system of recommendations by merit and was sold in bookshops for seven francs.

following dessert, a special
selection of sweet deliciousness
will arrive with coffee.

Speed, precision, skill and
energy: 2 p.m. in the kitchen
of the Ritz Hotel, Paris.

Restaurants were inspected anonymously and rated on a three-star system. Today the highest rating – three stars – means an exceptional standard of food, a very serious wine list, impeccable service and a journey well worth making. In France, a favourable assessment from Michelin is fundamental for chefs who want to rise through the ranks. The addition or loss of a star can mean the difference between financial success and failure.

In many French restaurants, Michelin-starred or not, the chef will be responsible for every aspect of the dining room as part of his overall domain; the flowers, the china, the glasses, the cutlery and the linen will all have had the chef's personal input. Very often it is a husband-and-wife team who work together to create this intimate atmosphere: she will supervise the front of house and he will orchestrate the cuisine. An extensive cellar will have evolved over decades. The partnership between sommelier and chef is close; the food and wine must balance each other. Even the design of the menu and wine list may have been commissioned from a local artist.

There are often unexpected flourishes when dining in France. The meal will start with an *amuse bouche* (surprise taster) from the kitchen: perhaps a mushroom-and-truffle soup or a salmon-and-crème-fraîche tartlet to stimulate the tastebuds and prepare the stomach. Following dessert, a special selection of sweet deliciousness will arrive with coffee: it might be miniature *millefeuille*, fruit jellies or bite-sized frozen sorbets and ice-creams. Not on the menu, these are a warm gesture of hospitality and an indication that the restaurant takes your appetite seriously.

At the end of an evening the chef will often enter the dining room to soft applause and a toast of '*Bravo! Bravo!*' Stopping at each table, sometimes accepting the offer of a *verre de vin* (glass of wine), he will lap up the praise for his evening's endeavours. He will have the undivided attention of each table. He might compliment the table on the vintage of wine they have chosen or recommend a dessert wine to follow. Aspects of the meal will be discussed. Everyone will pass an opinion, ask for details of the cooking method or praise him for the lightness of his sauce. French chefs work under extreme pressure, and night after night they must live up to their diners' expectations.

Their artistic talent and skill is worshipped by a nation. ❖

french chefs work under extreme
pressure, and night after night
they must live up to their

*L**A FERIA DE PÂQUES*** (Easter festival) in Arles runs for three or four days over the holiday period. This town, thirty minutes by car from Saint-Rémy-de-Provence, and with a population of 52 000, dates back to the seventh century BC and was a major Gallo-Roman city. Arles sits above the banks of the Rhône near where the river branches in two and flows to the Mediterranean. During Easter, celebrations are held morning, noon and night to mark the beginning of the bullfighting season, for this is a major spectator sport in south-western France. The bullfights are held in the Roman amphitheatre, which holds 12 000 people and is generally filled for each performance.

There are two types of bullfight. To participate in the *corrida*, the bulls must be at least four years old, and only fully qualified matadors may fight them. The *novillada* is for less-experienced matadors and younger, smaller and less-dangerous bulls. The apprentice matador must win many of these fights to graduate to the *corrida*. The bulls never graduate. David has reserved tickets for Paddy, himself and me to watch the *corrida*, while Emily and Venetia have said they would prefer to explore the town for the afternoon.

Reluctantly I climb to my place in the amphitheatre. On horseback, matador Juan Bautista enters the arena reminiscent of Louis XIV with flowing blond hair billowing behind him and a heavily brocaded jacket open to the waist. Handsome and young, he enthuses and seduces the crowd like a superstar. His dappled white horse dances to his touch and seems to turn on the space of a *centime* (French cent). The crowd starts clapping, slowly at first as he rides around the arena and then gradually faster and faster as they become impatient to sight the bull. An impressive beast bursts into the ring and a heavy silence descends. Together horse and matador are one against the bull. I know the odds and have hardened myself for

During Easter, celebrations
are held morning, noon and night
to mark the beginning of the
bullfighting season.

The Roman amphitheatre
in Arles.

the outcome. What I am not prepared for are the delicate and precise moves of the horse, the speed and learned skill of the matador and the energy of the crowd as they witness the bull's demise. The courtship between matador and bull is drawn out and intense; the subsequent conquest, fast and clean. Suddenly the arena is filled with white handkerchiefs waving back and forth – the crowd has awarded Juan Bautista the ultimate accolade for his horsemanship and bullfighting skills.

It is exciting and colourful, tragic and magnificent, gory and archaic all at the same time. It is also theatre.

To sit on massive stone blocks, many tiers high, in a living Roman amphitheatre among thousands of years of history is a remarkable experience.

As part of the Easter festivities, along with the bullfighting, there are extra street markets, concerts and theatre programs. This evening we meet up with the girls and dine at the Grand Hotel Nord-Pinus on the Place du Forum. A small hotel now classified as a national monument, it faces out onto a statue of famed Provençal writer Frédéric Mistral. Decorated with old posters of past bullfights, Nord-Pinus is the spot to catch a glimpse of today's matadors relaxing after their performance.

Around the square local shopkeepers have dressed and decorated their windows with traditional, colourful matador memorabilia, in keeping with the town's vibrant mood. Hot pink and acid yellow costumes alongside vermillion capes enliven the night. Café Van Gogh, renovated to look as it did in the painting *The Café Terrace on the Place du Forum, Arles at Night*, is packed with diners happy to bathe in the blue-and-yellow atmosphere.

The square and surrounding streets are heaving with Arlesiennes. There is an air of anticipation: the Gypsy Kings will be performing live to mark the *feria*. This group, originating from the gypsy community in Arles and Montpellier, mix moody vocals with acoustic guitars; their music is like a cross between flamenco and rumba.

Tonight is for dancing. The Place de la République glows in the evening light. The sky is clear and brilliant with stars. Suddenly a single sound shatters the stillness. One by one

Richly embroidered
matador's costume, Arles.

the guitarists take up the harmony, strumming slowly and melodiously. The notes seem to float and drift as they bounce back and forth off the stone walls. The crowd starts to move as the Latin rhythm picks up tempo. By the time the Kings play their most famous song, 'Bamboleo', the atmosphere is electric. They may have played concerts and dominated music charts all over the world, but this is their home town. They play encore after encore.

THE SATURDAY MARKET in Arles is enormous, and even more so at Easter time. There are stalls full of jewellery and clothing, china and lace, olives and tapenades, dried fruits, biscuits and pastries, handmade soaps and candles and spices of every colour. Chickens and ducks cackle noisily in their cages. Massive pans of saffron-coloured prawn paella simmer on the street corner, and the mobile pizza man (his van is equipped with a high-temperature oven) throws and stretches his dough ready for the lunchtime rush. The sight of a tomato-and-olive pizza fresh from the oven is impossible to ignore: the combination of its thin base, slightly crunchy in parts, with fresh tomato puree and black olives, seasoned with the traditional herbs of Provence, is heavenly. Another van is kitted with a rotisserie; the chickens turn until golden brown and are then bagged with their own juices over a vegetable ratatouille.

Seasonal produce features heavily in country markets. Boxes of asparagus, baskets of beans and trays of artichokes are everywhere. Among this vegetable concerto I spot some strawberries, large in size and rosy-red in colour. To my unprofessional eye they appear superb — a little early in the season, but tempting all the same. I select a basketful and search for my wallet. A local woman looks at me in kindly despair. Turning towards me, and with some gentle persuasion, she rests her fingers on my arm below the elbow. 'They are grown in Spain, they are Spanish,' she whispers. 'Spanish,' she says again from the corner of her mouth, eyes flashing, as if that is explanation enough.

fresh garlic from Wednesday's market, plaited and woven, decorates the kitchen table at Easter.

Summer breakfast: crusty baguettes and croissants with apricot jam or lavender honey; coconut yoghurt and white peaches garnished with mint from the garden, all set out on my mother's embroidered linens.

I feel like a small child as I set them back down, chastised yet unsure why. 'Wait another month until the home-grown strawberries and other red fruits have ripened,' she explains with a knowing glance. Be patient and respect the natural harmony of rural life.

THE COUNTRY takes on a relaxed mood as the temperatures soar during July and August. Saint-Rémy-de-Provence changes step to accommodate part-time residents from all over the world. The restaurants are bustling, cafe tables and chairs line the streets, small boutiques are open all weekend and buskers liven up the atmosphere at Wednesday's market. Visitors flock to lavender fields and scenic hilltop villages while music festivals dominate the calendar.

The days are long in summer. The light is intense and the heat desert-dry. Our farm is blessed with an abundance of water, so the velvet richness of the grass and the sound of running water cool the *mas*.

Excursions during the summer tend to be early morning or late afternoon to keep in step with the heat. Thursday mornings I like to visit Maussane and shop for the coming weekend. The market there is often less crowded than Saint-Remy's and has a wonderful selection of fruit, especially the local melons from Cavaillon. Venetia generally comes with me each week to see what's new with the local jewellery designers, and friends love the quilted bed coverings, matching tablecloths and napkins. Paddy prefers to stay home with David, to tear around the farm on his motorbike or race along the dirt tracks on the quad bike.

The ten-minute drive to Maussane on the winding D5 road slices through the Alpilles mountains, past Glanum. The natural vegetation – a spiky mixture of oak, pine, wild rosemary and thyme – is hardy and manages to survive with little water among the limestone. Once we drive through the mountains the view unfolds to reveal a plain filled with rows of vines and fields of established olive and almond trees.

Mausanne's morning market behind the main road is in full swing and the town square is filling up. Two cafes are the focus of the square, sitting side-by-side under umbrella-style plane trees. The only distinguishable difference between them is the colour of their cushions and umbrellas: one red, the other blue. The church bells are chiming and the gargoyle

MY FRENCH LIFE *à la campagne*

The village of Les-Baux-de-Provence sits below the ruins of the citadel. Narrow stone streets wind their way past museums and galleries to the escarpment above.

sculptures on the fountain spurt cool water. I always sit at the blue Café de la Fontaine. While Venetia is at the market I order a *café crème* and wander off to the *pâtisserie* next door. This French practice of buying pastries elsewhere and taking them to eat with your coffee at a bar or cafe is, I have learned, perfectly acceptable. The proprietors take no offence and will more than likely offer suggestions of which bakery is best. After a leisurely breakfast, I collect the weekend supplies, find Venetia and head home.

As we laze away the afternoon, gliders circle overhead, surfing the thermal winds. The Aero-Club de Saint Rémy les Alpilles sits in the foothills five minutes from Mas de Bérard. The wide, open landscape, clear skies and spectacular chain of mountains make this one of the most popular gliding destinations in Europe. Sleek fibreglass gliders are winched by tractor along a grass-covered runway and flung into the blue. As they hover and sweep they make their own distinct sound: a high-pitched birdsong resulting from a combination of movement and wind pockets. Today there is an acrobatic competition. Above us, gliders perform 360-degree loops, barrel rolls and deep plummets.

This funny little aerodrome reminds me so much of an Australian surf club. There are the old-timers whiling away their days, making it their home away from home. Stretched out on chairs, they gaze out to the sky instead of the sea. Weather-burned faces, lined and cracked, tell their tale. Enjoying the camaraderie of mates, they chat about the air currents and the flying conditions. Are they good or bad? How long will the gliders remain aloft? What distance will they cover? They sit watching and speculating over all the new kids on the block, hour after hour. They reminisce about all the pretty young things and they love to admire and trade tales with the young guns. Each evening after sunset the gliders are wheeled to their hangars, the logbooks recorded, and everyone relaxes as the *apéritif* hour kicks in.

My daughter Emily learned to fly this summer and is ready to solo. Every time I look up towards the Alpilles my heart is in my mouth as I watch her sweep overhead. I can barely breathe, so filled am I with that mother's dread and sickly anxiety.

Nearby, the dramatic fortress of Les Baux sits on a ridge of the Alpilles. Built in the tenth century by the Lords of Baux, this citadel overlooks a jagged gorge named the *Val d'Enfer* (Valley of Hell), said to have been the inspiration for some of Dante's poetry.

Once we drive through the mountains the view unfolds to reveal a plain filled with rows of vines and fields of established olive and almond trees.

Lying underneath this rugged landscape is a disused quarry, home to the dramatic sound-and-vision spectacular, Cathédrale d'Images. Made up of three main galleries, it was opened to the public in 1977. Although it is late afternoon, the temperature is still in the high 30s. As David and I enter this cavernous limestone quarry, it is immediately cool and dark, and we are grateful for the blankets given to us at the ticket office. Feeling our way along the tunnels, suddenly the walls are ablaze with Chinese characters and echo with the sound of Oriental music. Reflected on every surface of the 4000m² area are photographs of China: wall, ceiling and floor are alive with 2000–3000 colour images of the people, history and landscapes. With more than fifty projectors, each changing every thirty seconds, the slides create a moving audio-visual journey. This is an extraordinary and unpredictable feast deep within the quarry.

SUMMERTIME IN THE FRENCH COUNTRYSIDE is the smell of ripening fig trees and the taste of wild blackberries. It is the season for fruit picking: apples and pears to make juices and jams, vine-ripened tomatoes and wild strawberries. They are the months to invite friends and see the sights, or lay by the pool and read the latest novel. It is rare moments with our children, away from the distraction of the city and the pressures of school and university life. It is the time to take walks in the late afternoon and marvel at the dragonflies as they flit in and out of the grass along the banks of the canal. August is a month to close the shutters against the heat, listen to the cicadas and stay close to home.

As autumn approaches, the area of our garden we call 'the park' is radiant with colour. The rich green leaves of summer have turned to copper and bronze. The olives are ripening and we are preparing for the harvest. During the springtime the olive trees have blossomed and their fragrant white flowers have scattered in the wind. A week of fine, clear

days and steady mistral ensured a good number of the flowers were pollinated. During the summer the fruits have fattened with the scorching temperatures. The stones inside have hardened and the olives have begun to produce their oil. Further ripening means that by late November their colour has changed from a soft khaki to a rich aubergine.

By December, our neighbour's fields are rife with activity. Up and down the many avenues of olive trees, pickers are beginning to harvest. Men and women, balanced on ladders, strip the laden trees using wide-toothed combs. Nets underneath each tree quickly become full with the tumbling olives.

Our commercial trees are still young enough to be picked by hand and bear only small quantities of fruit. It is a very chilly morning even though the sun is shining. Rugged up against the cold, David and I commence with the fields closest to the house, helped by Christiane and Gérard.

The olives are full and plump, ready to fall. A single downwards action with both hands directs the fruit into a basket strapped around the waist. There is something comforting in this repetition; it is a peaceful process. The hours tick by and the crates fill up.

We sell our fruit to a local mill in Les-Baux-de-Provence. Castelas has been the recipient of a number of awards in the last few years. Their oil is evocative of the Alpilles: it smells of fresh grass and olives, tastes of sweet almond trees and raw artichokes and finishes with a peppery bite, suggesting the olives were fully ripe before pressing. The texture is fine, the colour a transparent citrus green and the taste sheer bliss.

Olive oil is like wine: the nose varies from the first taste on the palette, to the last remaining mouthful. A key ingredient of a richly flavoured olive oil is pressing the fruit within twenty-four hours of harvesting. When we arrive with our daily haul, the mill is noisy with the sound of machinery — it runs twenty-four hours a day, seven days a week and stops only when the very last olive has been picked and pressed. The air inside is moist with a fine

olive mist that permeates the air and saturates our hands and faces. My skin feels strangely soft and silken after a long day of tiring physical exertion.

Planting, nurturing and watching the olives grow has become my passion. They are a giant canvas, forever changing. Born and bred in the city, I am amazed at how rural charm has claimed me. I am staggered and surprised by my interest in farming talk and my desire to engage in it with other olive-growers. I enjoy nothing more than calling in at Castelas and chatting with Jean-Benoît Hugues, the proprietor, for an hour or two. We talk of the varieties and the pruning techniques, harvesting methods for the future and types of fertilisers for best growth. He laughs at my obsession with perfectly mown avenues of grass between the rows of olives, reminding me of the wear and tear on the tractor and the waste of fuel. I explain that this is my form of gardening, the precise order is beauty to my eyes. I am constantly shocked at my strange and unfamiliar behaviour – this was the girl who could find blindfolded any major shopping street in most capital cities and who came alive at the sound of honking horns and the first sight of a crowded avenue or boulevard. Now I find peace and contentment in my living sculptures where once I craved the buzz and constant adrenalin of the city.

The harvest is over, the oil pressed and winter is upon us. The leaves have vanished and the landscape appears doubled in size. The limestone peaks of Mont Ventoux are covered in snow and our mountains are reflecting metallic shadows in the low winter light. The village has re-awakened for the Christmas and New Year period. Festive lights dress the naked plane trees.

OUR NEIGHBOUR, Monsieur Guyot, has a posse of hunting dogs that wake me very early most mornings. With barks much worse than their bites, the slightest movement sends them off into a cacophony of howls and wails. Sometimes they escape into our fields and the mere sight

In Provence, weather, like life,
is more often than not theatrical.
When it rains it really rains,
when it is hot it scorches, and
when it is dry it bakes.

of our dogs Charlie and Nellie sends them scampering home at lightning speed: stealth and bravery are not part of their working credentials.

During the night I will often hear the hunters' shots and occasionally find evidence of the empty gun shells in the morning. I suspect they target the wild boar and the native birds that live in the foothills of the Alpilles. The locals short-cut up our driveway, cross over the canal, walk behind the house and pass through our olive fields, despite the many '*Defense d'entrer*' (Do not enter) signs and the yelps from the next-door pups.

IN PROVENCE, WEATHER, like life, is more often than not theatrical. When it rains it really rains, when it is hot it scorches, and when it is dry it bakes. Our life in the country turns on the seasons. Springtime is a time of blossom and mistral winds. Summer is the scent of lavender and the feel of intense heat. Autumn is a blaze of red and gold falling leaves, the olive harvest and oil press. Winter, my favourite season, is a quiet, peaceful time to unwind, relax and explore; the pause before the cycle of country life turns again. ✤

çaise

MARSEILLE PROVENCE INTERNATIONAL AIRPORT has that look of any major international airport: plenty of stern-looking guards at the kerb on arrival, and paired male and female security teams roaming throughout the terminal. The airport is always full of an eclectic crowd due to the proximity of North Africa. Atlas exotics such as Casablanca, Marrakech, Algiers and Tunis are some of the popular destinations announced over the intercom system.

Tourists are weighed down with their lasting impressions of Provence, straggling with too much carry-on as they try to push the limits of their baggage allowance. Cumbersome souvenir bags are secreted into the hands of their fidgeting children standing well behind the high-topped counters.

North Africans are wonderfully colourful travellers. They seem never to travel alone or pack a standard suitcase. Large square bundles of checked plastic straining at the seams somehow find their way into the hold without breaking; their hand luggage looks equally onerous. Dressed in flowing robes and matching headgear, they add flavour and excitement to the flying experience. The French business commuters are more reserved in their suits, standard-issue beige trench coats and shabby leather briefcases.

We are a mixed bunch as we proceed from the check-in counters to security. The brisk, efficient travellers of the world, the happy-go-lucky holiday-makers and the emotional first-timers are all thrown together.

I have learned queuing patience over the years, and I now relax into 'Provençal time', knowing my turn will eventually come. I travel light, unlike my fellow travellers who I watch charge in and out of the metal detectors, never seeming to understand they have to divest themselves of *all* metal objects and suspect paraphernalia. Belts, shoes, walking canes, hats and jewellery slowly come off one by one. As I mentally move towards London I start to repeat the mantra: patience is a virtue, patience is a virtue.

Feeling pressed for time, I present my boarding pass, lay my handbag on the conveyor belt and step through the silver security tunnel. At the same time I quietly contemplate a coffee and some magazines from the *presse* (newsagent) for the journey. As I reach for my bag all proceedings come to a very abrupt halt. A rapid discussion breaks out in French between the officials, but it is far too fast for me to understand. The larger of the two uniformed men stares me straight in the eyes and demands to know if I am the owner of this *sac* (bag). All thoughts of impatience are replaced with a nervous, undivided attention. I admit that the bag is mine, silently wondering what pair of scissors or nail file I have forgotten to remove. (How strange it is that we immediately feel guilty at the first sign of authority.) He halts the stream of passengers with a raised arm and a loud, '*Attendez-vous*' (Wait, please).

'Do you understand what is that bag?' he says now in faltering English.

By this time I am not only completely puzzled but quietly worried. I muster up my best, my most polite French in the hope of getting him onside: 'Excuse me, Monsieur, I am very sorry if I have made a terrible mistake, but I do not understand. What is it that I have done?'

He pauses for a moment, rotates his shoulders to correct his posture, stands tall and leans further towards me, forcing me to make eye contact with his piercing dark eyes. In absolute seriousness he replies, this time in French: 'Madame, let me explain something to you. Very simply, do you fully comprehend that this is one of the most magnificent, the most important and the most splendid handbags ever made in France? Are you aware, Madame, that you are a very, very fortunate woman to have this bag and that you must take very good care of it?'

His eyes soften as he stands the bag upright on its four tiny brass feet, peers inside and lovingly strokes the leather on each side. He is referring to my birthday present: a Birkin bag, by Hermès. He turns to his colleague, gives the signal to start the conveyor belt and waves me on. Where else in the world? He had true French style.

The French forge
together a combination
of intuition and daring,
a no-fear factor.

Sparkling eyes: this little
dog has the best seat on
the Métro.

Style is one of those inexplicable concepts that can mean every-thing and nothing at the same time. There is no formula or definition that encompasses *à la française* (French style). The French forge together a com-bination of intuition and daring, a no-fear factor. They have the ability to mix the most random elements and make them appear natural. Very few can duplicate it. It is unpredictable and I often wish I could bottle it.

Who can say why they do things the way they do? The old woman on the Métro carrying her dog in a leather handbag. Those famous red lips. The Ritz Hotel in Paris — chandeliers, silk taffeta curtains and maids wearing ballet pumps and white frilly aprons. The colour combinations — acid hues with aubergine, chartreuse and mauve. Converse boots and combat trousers. A 1-inch fringe and hacked gamine haircut. Hubert de Givenchy and the little black dress.

CHEZ PAUL ON THE RUE DE CHARONNE, in the eleventh arrondissement, is one of those Parisian institutions. Loaded with style, the smoke-stained walls and checked table-cloths make for a typical scene. Lace curtains, red bistro chairs and an ornate pressed-tin ceiling only add to the picture. Carla and I often eat here when we are together in Paris; it is an easy walk through the Place de la Bastille from her apartment in le Marais.

We are shown to our table by a voluptuous young woman who has that indescrib-able something about her. Her debut is minimal and efficient as she explains the specials in her clipped Parisian French. I admire the confidence of a young guy who is happy to forgo his main course and order only a chocolate lunch. Looking entirely content, he sits alone, nodding the occasional *bonjour* here and there. He is obviously a regular.

The wood-panelled bar sweeps from one side of the restaurant to the other. An enormous bunch of orange lilies sits on one end and an ice-filled champagne bucket on the other; in the middle the waitresses congregate when they're not serving tables. The size of a half-gallon drum, the bucket is stacked with bottles of the house *apéritif*. I cannot help but notice the man behind the bar talking on the telephone. He is wearing large round eyeglasses,

Morning preparations in the
Coco Chanel suite at the Ritz.
Style takes time;
the French make time.

*Valérie and Daniel
at Chez Paul.*

almost a caricature, with tortoiseshell arms that connect in a dead-straight line from the top of the cheekbone to the ears. He looks fantastic, very quirky and decidedly cool. He is the owner.

As we munch our way through a salad of fresh beetroot and green leaves, a commotion breaks out behind the bar. We can see that it revolves around a telephone conversation, but that is all. The telephone is black bakelite, standard French issue in the 1950s, with a round dial that turns clockwise and pings back as the number registers. Attached to the back of the handset is a device known as the 'mother-in-law listener', a cup that extends out on a stretch braid and enables a second person to hear the conversation. It appears that everyone is having a turn listening or speaking. There is much shaking of heads and swapping the handset between them. They keep hanging up and the caller keeps ringing back.

The same capable and professional girl returns to our table with the main course, but now she is angling for conversation. She fluffs our napkins, grinds pepper, chases mustard and offers wine. We do not really understand the turnaround. The others at the bar are watching and egging her on. She returns to them only to be sent back to our table. Meanwhile the telephone keeps ringing off the hook.

She discreetly bends to ear level and explains politely in vocabulary I understand that they have a problem and need my help in translating. Could I please come to the bar and speak to the owner? Apparently a non-French-speaking customer is continuing to call and they do not understand at all what he is saying. Chez Paul must be one of the only restaurants in Paris where English is not spoken – I am certain more through shyness and timidity than inability.

Naturally the caller is after a reservation, but for when and how many?

The long-suffering man calls back. I explain the situation – the owner listens in on the second earpiece – and I make the booking. In this amusing little cameo the whole restaurant becomes one. The ringing phone is suddenly a curiosity rather than an annoyance. The performance and production of asking for help and solving a problem immerses us all. The drama is pure French style.

The owner of
Chez Paul

The french have the ability to mix the most random elements and make them appear natural.

SPA SALOON AND ITALIAN TERRACE SCARBOROUGH

*Porcelain pups found
in the market at Barjac.*

SOMETIME DURING THE YEAR in most villages throughout France, there will be a *vide grenier* or *brocante*. The words translate as 'empty the attic' and 'second-hand goods', but they are much more than this. They are an excuse for a social day out and the chance to reshuffle old favourites. True French style.

Each August in the small town of Barjac in the Gard region, there is a weekend fair that attracts dealers and collectors from all over Provence. Barjac is a Renaissance town situated between the Cèze river gorges and the Ardèche, with extensive views of the Cévennes mountains. The whole town prepares for this fair: the restaurants and cafes double in size with outdoor tables; nearby fields are turned into parking areas; and the streets are closed to traffic to become one large open-air market. Several hours driving means an early start for Venetia and me to avoid the heat.

Stands have been constructed with everything from old trestle tables, sofas and chairs to Persian-style carpets. Each *marchand* (stallholder) stamps their personality on their makeshift home for the duration of the fair. Couples set themselves up with comfortable seating, plenty of reading matter, and food and wine for the slow times. Curtains are even hung on rickety poles and, of course, the pooch's security and wellbeing are attended to. The stalls display all sorts of wares, from large-scale furniture to minute memorabilia. There are stalls full of ex-military gear such as water bottles, compasses and army fatigues, and others are stacked with cutlery canteens with knives, forks and spoons in the hundreds. Porcelain dolls old enough to have slowly clicking eyes and long, curled eye-lashes stand in line. Sixties schoolroom charts from science and mathematics lessons hang above shelves filled with books. Chandeliers, candlesticks and retro lava lamps stand together, oblivious to the centuries of difference between them. Vintage clothes, make-up and perfume bottles shout for attention among feathers and fur. Dress-ups for grown-ups.

The larger furniture is exhibited in one street running down towards the bottom of the town. Four-poster beds, commodes and armoires are on display, fully made up with embroidered linens and placed against tapestry wall hangings. It is surreal to see these re-creations outside in the broad daylight.

Two customers, heads together, are measuring the length of an oak dining table. Calculating aloud, she is certain of fit. He, on the other hand, is unable to find any merit in the piece, begins to look bored, shuffles his feet, taps one toe a little and makes it very clear he wants to leave. Oblivious to us and presuming we don't understand French, they start a very vocal argument, accusing each other of all sorts of misdemeanours. (Funnily enough, it seems to be the same tune the world over between couples when shopping.) Clearly she would really like to buy the table, and clearly he is reluctant to part with the money. A little more bad behaviour and he storms off. She fights back tears, apologises to the dealer then leaves. Twenty minutes later they return hand-in-hand with smiles on their faces. The tears have miraculously vanished and the couple display the comfortable togetherness of a happy reconciliation. They start to haggle for the table, this time united in their advance. The dealer, who originally had all the bravado in the world, finally caves in under the protracted pressure and allows them to buy the table for well less than the asking price. I suspect this stylish performance was an elaborate ruse and a well-rehearsed act.

Meanwhile, my eyes rest on a pair of exquisite washed-out taupe linen sheets. Hand-embroidered linens were traditionally part of a marriage trousseau – pillowcases, the bolster cover, sheets and even nightdresses and petticoats would be hand-sewn by the bride with her initials. I could never understand why these magnificent collections, very often unused, would be put up for sale. The French seem to prefer new linens and those monogrammed only with their initials. I, on the other hand, love the detail of the intricate work. To me, the idea of the hours spent by a young girl to meticulously create her future seems romantic and something that should be preserved; a private pass into a long-forgotten world. I am gradually filling my own armoire with these old-fashioned hopes and dreams. Restored to their former glory, they are bleached and starched ready for a new life.

La mode française is all about a people in love with the pleasure of life, passionate and not afraid to show it, where individuality is revered and creativity much encouraged.

Style takes time; the French make time. ✣

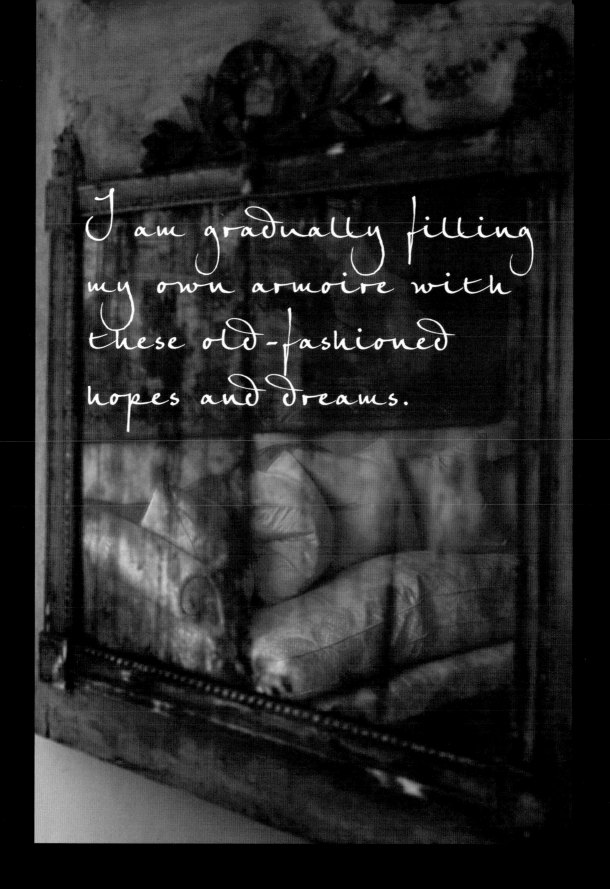

I am gradually filling my own armoire with these old-fashioned hopes and dreams.

COLOUR

FRENCH LIFE IS VIBRANT. It is colourful as much for the people as for the surroundings. Deep, full, rich colour, whether in the city or in the country, sets it apart. This is a life full of unexpected happenings and monumental surprises.

There is nothing like the shock of sunflowers stretching out toward the horizon on the drive to Arles or the jewel-like patchwork of lavender snaking through the hills toward Sault. The rose-coloured light of a Parisian evening is equally as enchanting as the blue haze of the Alpilles in that brief moment before the sun sets. Feathers flutter and diamantes glisten as the curtain goes up at the Moulin Rouge. The provincial markets and towns are full of unforgettable faces, and the city is enlivened by her many eccentric characters.

Life has sparkle.

I will never forget my first experience of a changing vineyard, long before we bought Mas de Bérard. I remember those vines, those colours as my turning point, the moment I first fell in love with France. Nestled in this vineyard near Saint-Tropez, the children and I went about our daily lives. Our time there was marked by the rich grassy greens of the hillsides and the old gold, tangerine and auburn shades of evolving leaves. Walking each day and exploring these surroundings, I learned the meaning of contentment. I felt calm and serene. The restless spirit that had always plagued me took a well-earned break. As the grapes grew and ripened, their violet richness came to symbolise the end of our holiday. Although filled with a poignant sadness that our carefree days were slipping away, I came to see the holiday as a new beginning.

Living here had introduced the possibility of a different life. I was seduced by the landscape and intrigued by the people. The language, the customs and the history seeped into my subconscious. Confusion and colour had entered my world.

The city is enlivened by her man

ccentric characters.

Red is the colour of the wild *coquelicots* (red poppies) that dust our fields in spring-time. Red is the glow of an evening sunset on a hot summer night or the swish of skirts swirling and twirling to the pump of a Latin beat. Red is the colour of flowering geraniums tumbling over the balconies of Paris. Red is luscious ripe strawberries in old-fashioned cartons. Red is the colour of our first tractor.

With the beginning of our life in France came a new era at Mas de Bérard; an old abandoned fruit farm has been given a second chance. As the farmhouse evolves and the olives grow, I am aware I too have changed.

When I think about the reasons why I find this French life irresistible, I am constantly aware that it is the unanticipated, the unforeseen and the adrenalin of unfamiliar circumstance. Every day becomes a new adventure — an adventure of language, custom and culture.

What is it that is so alluring about France? Why do so many people attempt to grasp the life and, in their way, become just a little bit French? I have met artists and lawyers, Australians and Americans, traders and architects, South Africans and English who have each fallen under the spell and made a love of all things French their passion. My passion for France endures. It began more than ten years ago and has held me captive ever since. When absent for any length of time I become conscious of the many varied elements I miss and how much I crave them. These elements are so fundamental to my life now that I think in some way they provide the key to this fascination.

I miss the smell of freshly baked baguettes and sitting down for lunch. Tearing the end off the still-warm breakfast loaf and munching it is a truly infectious French habit.

I miss the largeness of the sky and the noise of the cicadas. I miss the dusty, dry heat of summer and the numbing cold of winter. I miss blowing cigarette curls of frost on a bitterly cold January morning and the blast of heat that shocks and envelops the body like a blanket in mid-August.

I miss the soft crunch of gravel in the Jardin des Tuileries and the formation of sharp box hedges at the Hôtel des Invalides.

Lunch is a daily ritual of togetherness, a companionable celebration of food and real eating pleasure.

I miss the Provençal idea of time, the need for patience and adherence to local folklore. It becomes infectious, this slow, calculated order of decision-making. I miss wild thyme and rosemary perfuming the breeze and the sedation of heady lavender summers; the scents that seep in the upstairs windows at night are a recipe for sweet dreams. I miss the way the year is marked by the seasons — memories are triggered by what happened two winters ago, or by the eleven-day mistral last Easter. I miss the worn hues of the shutters and the faded advertisements that tattoo the older establishments. I miss the hilltop villages and their daily markets. The Roman ruins and their history are centuries of past life only moments away. I miss the beach clubs of the Mediterranean and the bouillabaisse of Marseille.

Nowhere else will you find the shrug of the shoulder, the tilt of the head and the little puff of air that regularly escapes a Frenchman's mouth, or the formality of good wishes that introduce every conversation. That sense of style that permeates everything from interiors to individuals, and is everywhere I look. The eccentricity of the films and the zany music that is so eclectic but also endearing. That extra *bisou* (kiss) hello in the south seems to say it all. Welcome to Provence: larger-than-life greetings, larger-than-life landscapes and larger-than-life characters.

I miss the architectural uniformity and the grandeur that is Paris; the broad avenues, the cobbled backstreets, the police sirens and the fanatic drivers are a familiar tableau. I miss Christmas decorations at the Place Vendôme, window-shopping around the Rue du Faubourg Saint-Honoré and the kilometres of fairy lights that wrap the Champs Élysées. I miss the perfumeries and other speciality shops: the mustard shop, the violin-maker's shop and the vintage shops are wonders in this day of homogenous marketing and designer dictation. I miss the semicircle of female stone statues in the Jardin du Luxembourg and the show of tulips in the Palais Royal. I miss shadow lines that play on the Seine at dusk and the soft glow of old-style street lamps. I miss the language: the cadence and the delicate nuances of the vocabulary.

Christmas decorations
at the Place Vendôme.

Venetia runs in the front door at Mas de Bérard, April 2005.

It is impossible to overlook the waiters and their nonchalance, the bistros, the brasseries, the cafes and the daily specials on the blackboard, the coloured cane chairs greeting the street and the guarantee of a table for as long as you want; relaxed coffee-drinking and people-watching is an addictive spectator sport. The penguin suits, the frilly aprons and the one-handed balancing act *are* Paris.

I miss macaroons, tarte tatin and roast chicken with chips. I miss nougat, caramels and soft peach-coloured rosé. I miss the long belted trench coats and battered leather briefcases that so typify this cityscape.

I miss the elegance of the Avenue Montaigne and the smartness of the Rue de Grenelle. I miss the age of the Marais *quartier*, the fluttering of the flags on the Colonne de Juillet at the Place de la Bastille and the liveliness of the tenth arrondissement. I miss the music in the Métro and the summer dancing in the streets. I miss the jumble and confusion of the flea markets, the small first-time exhibitions and the Centre Georges Pompidou. I even miss the dogs.

MID-JULY AND THE FIRST FLUSH of summer is still with us. The sound of the *chemin d'eau* (waterway) tinkles in the background, softening the song of the cicadas. Gliders are above, enjoying a slight breeze from the west, while the white rose petals dance and scatter their way over the lawn.

Saying goodbye to a group of our children's friends who have enjoyed a week-long celebration of Emily's twentieth birthday, I realise my dream has come true. Our home is filled with family and friends, and friends of family and their friends. We have a magnificent view overlooking the Alpilles, olives trees that continue to prosper and a garden that wraps the *mas* in serenity and calm. I have come to understand that making time and taking time is a pleasure to be enjoyed, not a nuisance to endure. Falling in love with this place all those years ago changed my life as I knew it; my *coup de foudre* opened the door to another life, my French life. ❖

my french address book

PARIS

Restaurants, cafes, clubs

Bal du Moulin Rouge
Montmartre
82 Boulevard de Clichy
75018 Paris
+33 1 53 09 82 82
www.moulin-rouge.com

Barrio Latino
46–48 Rue du Faubourg
Saint-Antoine
75012 Paris
+33 1 55 78 84 75

Brasserie Lipp
151 Boulevard Saint-Germain
75006 Paris
+33 1 45 48 72 93
www.brasserie-lipp.fr

Café de Flore
172 Boulevard Saint-Germain
75006 Paris
+33 1 45 48 55 26
www.cafe-de-flore.com

Chez André
12 Rue Marbeuf
75008 Paris
+33 1 47 20 59 57

Café Le Nemours
2 Galerie de Nemours
Place Colette
75001 Paris
+33 1 42 61 34 14

Les Deux Magots
6 Place Saint-Germain-des-Prés
75006 Paris
+33 1 45 48 55 25
www.lesdeuxmagots.fr

Les Éditeurs
4 Carrefour de l'Odéon
75006 Paris
+33 1 43 26 67 76

Restaurant Chez Paul
13 Rue de Charonne
75011 Paris
+33 1 47 00 34 57

Café Jacquemart-André
158 Boulevard Haussman
75008 Paris
+33 1 45 62 04 44

Café Marly
Palais du Louvre
93 Rue de Rivoli
+33 1 49 26 06 60

Restaurant Georges
Centre Georges Pompidou
Rue Saint-Martin
75004 Paris
+33 1 44 78 47 99

Ladurée
(Pâtisserie and tea room)
www.laduree.com

75 Avenue des Champs-Elysées
75008 Paris
+33 1 40 75 08 75

16 Rue Royale
75008 Paris
+33 1 42 60 21 79

21 Rue Bonaparte
75006 Paris
+33 1 44 07 64 87

62 Boulevard Haussmann
75009 Paris
+33 1 42 82 40 10

Antiquities and curiosities

Au Duc de Chartres
(Antique medals)
26 Galerie de Chartres
Jardin du Palais Royal
75001 Paris
+33 1 42 96 07 52

A l'Oriental
(Antique pipes)
19–22 Galerie de Chartres
Jardin du Palais Royal
75001 Paris
+33 1 42 96 43 16

Boîtes à Musique Anna Joliet
(Musical boxes)
9 Rue de Beaujolais
Jardins du Palais Royal
75001 Paris
+33 1 42 96 55 13
www.boitesamusiqueannajoliet.com

H. Picard & Fils
(Antique booksellers)
126 Rue du Faubourg-Saint-Honoré
75008 Paris
+33 1 43 59 28 11
www.antikaparis.com/picard

Les Drapeaux de France
(Antique toy soldiers)
13–14 Galerie Montepensier
Jardins du Palais Royal
75001 Paris
+33 1 42 97 55 40

Fashion

Boutique Chantal Thomass
(Lingerie)
211 Rue Saint-Honoré
75001 Paris
+33 1 42 60 40 56
www.chantalthomass.fr

Christian Louboutin
(Shoes)
38–40 Rue de Grenelle
75001 Paris
+33 1 42 22 33 07

Colette
(Style, design, art, food)
213 Rue Saint-Honoré
75001 Paris
+33 1 55 35 33 90
www.colette.fr

Destray Rive Gauche
(Optician)
40 Rue du Four
75006 Paris
+33 1 45 48 61 33

Goyard
(Luggage)
233 Rue Saint-Honoré
75001 Paris
+33 1 42 60 57 04
www.goyard.fr

Kabuki
(Designer clothes and accessories)
13 Rue de Turbigo
75002 Paris
+33 1 42 36 44 34

21 and 25 Rue Etienne Marcel
75001 Paris
+33 1 42 33 13 44
+33 1 42 33 55 65

L'Éclaireur
(Designer clothes and accessories)
www.leclaireur.com

10 Rue Hérold
75001 Paris
+33 1 40 41 09 89

131–133 Galerie de Valois
Jardins du Palais Royal
75001 Paris
+33 1 40 20 42 52

12 Rue Mahler
75004 Paris
+33 1 44 54 22 11

3 Rue des Rosiers
75004 Paris
+33 1 48 87 10 22

26 Avenue des Champs-Elysées
75008 Paris
+33 1 45 62 12 32

Pierre Hardy
(Shoes)
156 Galerie de Valois
Jardins du Palais Royal
75001 Paris
+33 1 42 60 59 75
www.pierrehardy.com

Roger Vivier
(Shoes)
29 Rue du Faubourg-Saint Honoré
75008 Paris
+33 1 53 43 00 00

Vintage

Didier Ludot
(Vintage clothing, accessories and
Didier Ludot's collection)
125 Galerie de Valois
Jardins du Palais Royal
75001 Paris
+33 1 40 15 01 04
www.didierludot.com

La Licorne
(Vintage jewellery)
38 Rue de Sévigné
75003 Paris
+33 1 48 87 84 43

**Scarlett Haute Couture Les
Antiquaires de la mode**
(Vintage clothing and accessories)
10 Rue Clément Marot
75008 Paris
+33 1 56 89 03 00
www.scarlett.fr

Books

Assouline Boutique
35 Rue Bonaparte
75006 Paris
+33 1 43 29 23 20
www.assouline.com

Taschen
2 Rue de Buci
75006 Paris
+33 1 40 51 79 22
www.taschen.com

BDNET
(Comics)
26 Rue de Charonne
75011 Paris
+33 1 43 55 50 50
www.bdnet.com

Department stores

BHV Rivoli
14 Rue du Temple
75189 Paris
+33 1 42 74 90 00
www.bhv.fr

Le Bon Marché
24 Rue de Sèvres
75007 Paris
+33 1 44 39 80 00
www.lebonmarche.fr

La Grande Épicerie
38 Rue de Sèvres
75007 Paris
+33 1 44 39 81 00
www.lagrandeepicerie.fr

La Samaritaine
19 Rue de la Monnaie
75001 Paris
+33 1 40 41 20 20
www.lasamaritaine.com

Les Galeries Lafayette Maison
40 Boulevard Haussmann
75009 Paris
+33 1 42 82 34 56
www.galerieslafayette.com

Hotels

Hôtel Costes
239 Rue Saint-Honoré
75001 Paris
+33 1 42 44 50 00
www.hotelcostes.com

Hôtel Plaza Athénée
25 Avenue Montaigne
75008 Paris
+33 1 53 67 66 65
www.plaza-athenee-paris.com

Ritz Hôtel
15 Place Vendôme
75001 Paris
+33 1 43 16 30 30
www.ritzparis.com

Scents

Annick Goutal Parfums Paris
www.annickgoutal.com

14 Rue de Castiglione
75001 Paris
+33 1 42 60 52 82

3 Rue des Rosiers
75004 Paris
+33 1 48 87 80 11

12 Place Saint Sulpice
75006 Paris
+33 1 46 33 03 15

Éditions de Parfums
Frédéric Malle
37 Rue de Grenelle
75007 Paris
+33 1 42 22 77 22
www.fredericmalle.com

140 Avenue Victor Hugo
75116 Paris
+33 1 45 05 39 02

Hervé Gambs
9 Rue des Blancs Manteaux
75004 Paris
+33 1 44 59 88 88
www.hervegambs.com

Les Salons du Palais Royal Shiseido
142 Galerie de Valois –
24 Rue de Valois
Jardin du Palais Royal
75001 Paris
+33 1 49 27 09 09
www.salons-shiseido.com

Lunx Parfums Paris
48–50 Rue de l'Université
75007 Paris
+33 1 45 44 50 14

Mathias Paris
117 Rue de Charenton
75012 Paris
+33 1 43 07 98 22
www.mathias-paris.com

Sephora
70–72 Avenue des Champs-Elysées
75008 Paris
+33 1 53 93 22 50

25 Rue de la République
84000 Avignon
+33 4 90 80 40 80
www.sephora.fr

Antique Markets Saint-Ouen
Métro: Porte de Clignancourt

Marché Paul Bert
(Furniture and decorative wares)
18 Rue Paul Bert
93400 Saint-Ouen
+33 1 40 11 54 14

Marché Serpette
(Furniture and decorative wares)
110 Rue des Rosiers
93400 Saint-Ouen
+33 1 40 11 54 14

Lili et Daniel
(Ribbons and trimmings)
Marché Vernaison
Stand 6 Allee 1
99 Rue des Rosiers
93400 Saint-Ouen
+33 1 40 12 01 24

Museums

Centre Georges Pompidou
Place Georges Pompidou
Rue Saint-Martin
75004 Paris
+33 1 44 78 12 33
www.centrepompidou.fr

Musée Jacquemart-André
158 Boulevard Haussmann
75008 Paris
+33 1 45 62 11 59
www.musee-jacquemart-andre.com

Musée du Louvre
34–36 Quai du Louvre
75001 Paris
+33 1 40 20 50 50
www.louvre.fr

Musée National Picasso
Hôtel Salé
5 Rue de Thorigny
75003 Paris
+33 1 42 71 25 21
www.musee-picasso.fr

Musée Rodin
Hôtel Biron
79 Rue de Varenne
75007 Paris
+33 1 44 18 61 10
www.musee-rodin.fr

At the beach

L'Eden
(Restaurant)
Plage Mala
Cap d'Ail
+33 4 93 78 17 06

La Reserve
(Restaurant)
Plage Mala
Cap d'Ail
+33 4 93 78 21 56

La Voile d'Or
(Hotel and restaurant)
7 Avenue Jean Mermoz
06230 Saint-Jean-Cap-Ferrat
+33 4 93 01 13 13
www.lavoiledor.fr

Hôtel Byblos
Avenue Paul Signac
83990 Saint-Tropez
+33 4 94 56 68 00
www.byblos.com

Le Club 55
(Restaurant and beach club)
43 Boulevard Patch
83350 Ramatuelle
+33 4 94 55 55 55

Senequier
(Cafe and patisserie)
Quai Jean Jaurès
Place aux Herbes
83990 Saint-Tropez
+33 4 94 97 00 90

Vilebrequin
(Swimwear for men)
Place de la Garonne
83990 Saint-Tropez
+33 4 94 43 33 46
www.vilebrequin.com

SAINT-RÉMY-DE-PROVENCE AND SURROUNDING VILLAGES

Actuel Immobilier
(Real estate agency)
7 Rue Lafayette
13210 Saint-Rémy-de-Provence
+33 4 32 60 16 62
www.actuelimmobilier.net

Aéro-Club
(Gliding club)
Saint-Rémy Les Alpilles
Aérodrome de Romanin
13210 Saint-Rémy-de-Provence
+33 4 90 92 08 43

Castelas
(Olive Oil producers)
Huile d'Olive AOC
De la Vallée des Baux-de-Provence
+33 4 90 54 50 86
www.castelas.com

Saint-Rémy Presse
(Newsagency and bookshop)
12 Boulevard Mirabeau
13210 Saint-Rémy-de-Provence
+33 4 90 92 05 36
www.saintremy.lalibrairie.com

Antiques and restoration

Château du Deffends
Hameau du Flayosquet
83780 Flayosc
+33 4 94 50 22 50

L'Atelier 13
Route de Graveson
13630 Eyragues
+33 4 90 24 94 19
www.antique-french-stone.com

Portes Anciennes
www.portesanciennes.com

Route d'Avignon
13210 Saint-Rémy-de-Provence
+33 4 90 92 13 13

Route Nationale 7
13670 Saint-Andiol
+33 4 90 95 02 89

Brasseries and restaurants

L'Aile ou la Cuisse
5 Rue de la Commune
13210 Saint-Rémy-de-Provence
+33 4 32 62 00 25

Grain de Sel
25 Boulevard Mirabeau
13210 Saint-Rémy-de-Provence
+33 4 90 92 00 89
www.graindesel-resto.com

Le Bistrot des Alpilles
15 Boulevard Mirabeau
13210 Saint-Rémy-de-Provence
+33 4 90 92 09 17

Brasserie Les Varietes
32 Boulevard Victor Hugo
13210 Saint-Rémy-de-Provence
+33 4 90 92 42 61

Café du Lézard
12 Boulevard Gambetta
13210 Saint-Rémy-de-Provence
+33 4 90 92 59 66

Hôtel Gounod – le salon de thé
Place de la République
13210 Saint-Rémy de Provence
+33 4 90 92 06 14
www.hotel-gounod.com

Le Bistrot d'Eygalières
Rue de la République
13810 Eygalières
+33 4 90 90 60 34
www.chezbru.com

L'Oustau de Baumanière
Val d'Enfer
13520 Les-Baux-de-Provence
+33 4 90 54 33 07
www.oustaudebaumaniere.com

Grand Hotel Nord Pinus
(Hotel and restaurant)
Place du Forum
13200 Arles
+33 4 90 93 44 44
www.nord-pinus.com

Food and wine

Boulangerie Banette
(Bakery)
Avenue de la Libération
13210 Saint-Rémy-de-Provence
+33 4 90 92 51 37

Charmeroy
(Tea shop)
26 Boulevard Mirabeau
13210 Saint-Rémy-de-Provence
+33 4 32 60 01 23
www.charmeroy.com

Glanum Pizza
(Pizzeria)
14 Boulevard Marceau
13210 Saint-Rémy-de-Provence
+33 4 90 92 24 29

Inter Caves
(Wine)
1 Avenue du 19 Mars 1962
13210 Saint-Rémy-de-Provence
+33 4 90 92 50 30
www.intercaves.fr

Joël Durand Chocolatiér
(Chocolate)
3 Boulevard Victor Hugo
13210 Saint-Rémy-de-Provence
+33 4 90 92 38 25

La Cure Gourmande
(Biscuits)
6 Rue de la Commune
13210 Saint-Rémy-de-Provence
+33 4 90 92 10 82

Le Petit Duc
(Biscuits)
7 Boulevard Victor Hugo
13210 Saint-Rémy-de-Provence
+33 4 90 92 08 31
www.petit-duc.com

Le Roma Artisan Glacier
(Ice-cream)
33 Boulevard Marceau
13210 Saint-Rémy-de-Provence
+33 4 90 92 14 33

Lilamand Confiseur
(Glazed fruit)
5 Avenue Albert Schweitzer
13210 Saint-Rémy-de-Provence
+33 4 90 92 12 77
www.lilamand.com

Olive Huiles du Monde
(Olive oil)
16 Boulevard Victor Hugo
13210 Saint-Rémy-de-Provence
+33 4 90 92 53 93

Poissonnerie Maureau
(Fishmonger)
22 Rue Carnot
13210 Saint-Rémy-de-Provence
+33 4 90 92 04 67

Agneau de Maussane
(Butcher)
55 Avenue de la Vallée des Baux
13520 Maussane-les-Alpilles
+33 4 90 54 34 88

Le Jardin des Alpilles
(Fruit and vegetables)
93 Avenue de la Vallée des Baux
13520 Maussane-les-Alpilles
+33 4 90 54 47 28

Vineyards

Domaine Hauvette
Chemin du Trou-des-Boeufs
La Haute Galine
13210 Saint-Rémy-de-Provence
+33 4 90 92 03 90

Chateau Romanin
13210 Saint-Rémy-de-Provence
+33 4 90 92 45 87
www.romanin.com

Domaine de Trevallon
13103 Saint-Etienne-du-Gres
+33 4 90 49 06 00
www.trevallon.com

Gifts and homeware

La Fabrique
(Basketware)
25 Avenue de la Libération
13210 Saint-Rémy-de-Provence
+33 4 90 92 02 27

Le Bazar Saint-Rémois
(Gifts)
1 Rue de la Commune
13210 Saint-Rémy-de-Provence
+33 4 90 26 90 72

Le Grand Magasin
(Jewellery and gifts)
24 Rue de la Commune
13210 Saint-Rémy-de-Provence
+33 4 90 92 18 79

N.M. Déco
(Homeware)
9 Rue Hoche
13210 Saint-Rémy-de-Provence
+33 4 90 92 57 91

Acanthe
(Homeware and gifts)
Route de Murs
83220 Gordes
+33 4 90 72 15 72

La Maison d'Anaïs
(Gifts)
Rue de la République
13810 Eygalières
+33 4 90 90 65 44

Florist

Aux Bouquet de July-Fleuriste
13210 Saint-Rémy-de-Provence
+33 4 90 92 62 99

Tourist information

Arles Billeterie
Arenès d'Arles
13633 Arles
+33 4 90 96 03 70
www.arenes-arles.com
www.ville-arles.fr/feria
www.tourisme.ville-arles.fr

Cathedrale d'Images
Route de Maillane
13520 Les-Baux-de-Provence
+33 4 90 54 38 65
www.cathedrale-images.com

Site archéologique de Glanum
Route des Baux-de-Provence
13210 Saint-Rémy-de-Provence
+33 4 90 92 23 79
www.monum.fr

The Cloister of Saint Paul Mausole
Route des Baux-de-Provence
13210 Saint-Rémy-de-Provence

Chorégies d'Orange
(Concerts and theatre)
18 Place Silvain
84100 Orange
+33 4 90 34 24 24
www.choregies.com

my french inspiration

FILMS

Beautifully photographed, with great sets and fabulous locations, these films provide a small insight into the French. Unlike most Hollywood blockbusters, they focus on the emotional journey rather than action and special effects. Plots with highly unpredictable twists and turns seem to dominate the screen.

L'Appartement starring Vincent Cassel and Monica Belluci
A mixture of love story and thriller set in Paris. Affairs of the heart, consoling conversations and a very emotional male character entwined in the fate of three gorgeous women. Max, the principal character, is simultaneously arranging a marriage, solving a murder, finding lost love and becoming involved with a mysterious female.

Merci pour le Chocolat starring Isabelle Huppert and Jacques Dutronc
A dark thriller that revolves around an intricate and murderous web of deception. Huppert plays the central character, the wife of a celebrated pianist, whose dark past of secrets and lies gradually unfolds.

Alice et Martin starring Juliette Binoche
A love story between two emotionally fragile people. Alice and Martin embark on an affair after meeting in the apartment she shares with his half-brother. As their relationship develops their happiness becomes short-lived when a shocking secret in Martin's past is revealed.

Comédie de l'Innocence starring Isabelle Huppert, Jeanne Balibar and Charles Berling
A psychological thriller involving two women who compete for the attention of the son they both call their own. On his ninth birthday Camille announces to his mother Ariane that he wants to return to his 'true' mother. What follows is a subtle, intriguing and suspenseful mystery.

Place Vendôme starring Catherine Deneuve
Marianne, played by Deneuve, rekindles her ambition to be a player in the international diamond trade after her husband's apparent death. Her realisation that his prestigious jewellery business is riddled with debt leads her into the dangerous underworld of the diamond trade, where she uncovers a sinister network of conspiracy and deception.

Les Soeurs Fâchées starring Isabelle Huppert and Catherine Frot
Two sisters, Louise and Martine, are completely different. Louise is a writer who lives in the country, while the elder Martine is beautiful, aloof and belongs in smart Parisian society. Louise visits her sister in Paris and becomes an embarrassment as she struggles to conceal her upbringing and hold her unhappy life together.

Boudu starring Gérard Depardieu, Gérard Jugnot and Catherine Frot
Chaos enters the life of gallery-owner Christian when, in an act of heroism, he saves Boudu from drowning himself in the waters of a canal. This comedy ends in complication and chaos when he feels a responsibility to the victim and is forced to shelter him.

Three Colours Blue starring Juliette Binoche
The first film in a trilogy commenting on contemporary French society. Set in the period just prior to the formation of the European Union, *Three Colours Blue* follows a woman dealing with the death of her husband and child in tragic circumstances.

Les Choristes starring Gérard Jugnot
Clémont, an unsuccessful composer, takes a position in a boarding school for difficult boys. He eventually finds a way to reach them through his music, only to be thwarted by the harsh disciplinarian code of the headmaster.

8 Femmes starring Catherine Deneuve, Isabelle Huppert, Emmanuelle Béart and Fanny Ardant
A French farce which, in the space of 106 minutes, entertains with love triangles, betrayals, murders and intrigue. Played by some of the great icons of French cinema, the eight women are feminine portraits on a grand stage. Lined up holding hands for the finale, as if on Broadway, the eight women fill the screen with that 'little French something'.

Chocolat starring Juliette Binoche and Johnny Depp
Although not a French production, this is a wonderful portrayal of French village life.

Indochine starring *Catherine Deneuve and Vincent Perez*
An epic drama of colonial life in Indochina during the 1930s. The film chronicles the relationship between a wealthy French plantation-owner and her adopted native daughter as their paths become intertwined with that of a young officer.

La Gloire de mon Père and Le Château de ma Mère starring *Phillipe Caubère and Nathalie Roussel*
These two films are based on the childhood of famous Provençal writer Marcel Pagnol. The family spend their holidays in the countryside and discover the joys of nature.

Jean de Florette and Manon des Sources starring *Yves Montand, Gérard Depardieu and Daniel Auteuil*
A city-dweller moves to the countryside of Provence to begin a new life as a farmer. His innocence and naïvety allow his neighbours to destroy him. Wonderfully photographed, this is a tale of greed, envy and revenge.

MUSIC

I enjoy listening to French music because it is eclectic and emotional; with great outpourings of sensitivity and colourful content, French music holds nothing back. There are the serious compositions, the quirky love songs and the ageing rockers who carry on crooning their melodies to all ages.

Here are some of my favourite songs and albums.

'Je t'aime . . . Moi non Plus' Jane Birkin and Serge Gainsbourg

'Couleur Café' Serge Gainsbourg

'Comic Strip' Serge Gainsbourg

'Love and the Beat' Serge Gainsbourg

'Monsieur Gainsbourg Revisited' Classic Gainsbourg reinterpreted by a selection of recording artists including Jarvis Cocker and Marianne Faithfull.

'Tout un Jour' Isabelle Boulay

'Quelqu'un m'a dit' Carla Bruni

'Les Chansons D'amour' Françoise Hardy

'Tant de Belles Choses' Françoise Hardy

'The Vogue Years' Françoise Hardy

'Les Choristes' Original music from the movie, composed and orchestrated by Bruno Coulais.

And then there are the composers, the great singers and interpreters of French songs.

'Infiniment: 40 chansons' Jacques Brel

'Le Disque D'or' Georges Brassens

'Les Indispensables De Léo Ferré' Léo Ferré

'Beaucoup de Bécaud: Best of' Gilbert Bécaud

'Double Enfance' Julien Clerc

'Les Indispensables de Barbara' Barbara

'Succes & Confidences' Serge Reggiani

'She: The best of Charles Aznavour' Charles Aznavour

'Un Gamin de Paris' Yves Montand

'Intégrale 1965–1995' Michel Sardou

'Chansons d'Edith Piaf', 'La Vie en rose' Edith Piaf

BOOKS

Historical accounts, adventure tales, short stories, local memoirs, exhibition catalogues and a homage to a national icon: here are a few books from and about France I could happily read again and again.

The Count of Monte Cristo by *Alexandre Dumas (Collins, 1988)*
This is my all-time adored tale of revenge written by one of France's best-known writers. Edmond Dantès, framed as a Napoleonic conspirator, plans a path of vengeance and retribution disguised as the enigmatic Count of Monte Cristo. This enormous saga sweeps from the backstreets of Marseille to the suburbs of Paris; a fast-paced adventure amalgamating fiction with dubious historical fact.

Napoleon and Josephine: A Love Story by *Theo Aronson (St Martins Press, 1991)*
This account of the French ruler's domestic life and marriage to Josephine de Beauharnais reads like a romantic novel. The relationship between Napoleon and Josephine was an attraction of opposites. Napoleon saw his wife as his good luck charm, and with her by his side he felt he could not fail. Coincidentally after their divorce the Empire crumbled. This absorbing read is an easy guide to the Napoleonic years.

Birdsong by *Sebastian Faulks (Vintage, 2005)*
In 1910 a young Englishman travels to Picardy in France and begins an affair with the wife of his employer. Several years later he finds himself in the fighting fields as a soldier on the Western Front after the outbreak of World War I. This emotive tale of war explores not only those who fought, but those whose lives were forever changed as a result. Superbly descriptive, this novel stays in the mind long after reading.

Suite Française by Irène Némirovsky
(Chatto & Windus, 2006)
Sixty-two years after the author died
in Auschwitz, this two-part work
(originally intended as a five-volume
epic), was published. 'Storm in June'
tells of the June 1940 evacuation
during which much of the French
population fled from the Nazi
invasion. 'Dolce' depicts the small
village of Bussy at the beginning of
the occupation. This newly released
work is considered by French critics
as a defining novel of their nation
during World War II.

French Ways and Their Meaning
by Edith Wharton (Berkshire House, 1997)
Mrs Wharton, by way of a sequence
of letters written for English and
American soldiers off to France
during World War I, attempts to
interpret the essence of the French
character from an American
viewpoint.

A Moveable Feast by Ernest Hemingway
(Authorhouse, 2003)
An account of Hemingway's early days
in Paris, with marvellous descriptions
of local characters and cafe life.
During the expatriate era in Paris,
Hemingway was surrounded by writers
such as F. Scott Fitzgerald, Gertrude
Stein and T.S. Eliot.

Paris Tales by Helen Constantin
(Oxford University Press, 2004)
A collection of stories by French
and Francophile writers, including
Colette, Maupassant and Nerval,
which allow the reader to steal a look
into Parisian life from the mid-
nineteenth century to today.

An English Garden in Provence
by Natasha Spender, Stephen Spender,
Jean-Marie Del Moral (Harvill Press, 1999)
Natasha Spender was one of the first
to write about the beauty of Provence
and her love for the region. This
book has become a record of the
Spenders' house and garden at Mas St
Jérome in the foothills of the Alpilles,
in Provence, which were later almost
completely burned to the ground by
a fierce bushfire.

A Year in Provence by Peter Mayle
(Penguin, 2000)
The original light-hearted memoir
of life in the south of France. There
is no doubt Peter Mayle changed the
face of Provence and opened the
region to tourists and foreign
homeowners. A record of a Provence
now past, it still resonates.

Jean Cocteau by Dominique Paini
(Centre Georges Pompidou, 2003)
This catalogue is from the 2003–
2004 retrospective devoted to this
French artist, writer, filmmaker and
poet. It is a comprehensive collection
of paintings, photographs, drawings
and film footage that illustrates
Cocteau's complex artistry.

*The World of Coco Chanel: Friends,
Fashion, Fame* by Edmonde Charles-Roux
(Thames & Hudson, 2005)
A gorgeous look at Gabrielle 'Coco'
Chanel, the most famous of French
fashion icons. This stylish book
is full of beautiful anecdotes and
photographs that bring back to
life the era of elegance created by
Coco Chanel.

Chanel by Harold Koda and Andrew Bolton
(Metropolitan Museum of Art, 2005)
A 2005 exhibition at the Costume
Institute of the Metropolitan Museum
of Art, New York, showcased the
history of the House of Chanel.
Period examples were mixed with

those of Karl Lagerfeld, who joined
the House of Chanel in 1983.
This smart linen-bound catalogue
from the exhibition highlights the
achievements of both with a series
of essays and photographs.

Books about architecture, decoration
and gardens have always filled my
shelves. I have an endless love of
interiors, and never tire of reading
about French décor and design. I find
sophisticated Parisian apartments and
humble Provençal farmhouses equally
fascinating. During the restoration of
Mas de Bérard I pored over countless
volumes in my search for ideas.
French magazines such as *Côté Sud*,
Maison Française and *Elle Décoration* were
an invaluable source of inspiration,
as were the following books.

Provence Interiors by Lisa Lovatt-Smith
(Taschen, 1997)

Living in Provence by Barbara and René
Stoeltie (Taschen, 2005)

Living in Provence by Dane McDowell and
Christian Sarramon (Flammarion, 2003)

The Provençal House by Johanna Thornycroft
and Andreas von Einsiedel (Skriptum Editions,
2003)

*New French Country: A Style and Source
Book* by Linda Dannenberg and Guy Bouchet
(Thames & Hudson, 2004)

*The French Touch: Decoration and Design
in the Most Beautiful Homes of France*
by Daphné de Saint Sauveur (Thames &
Hudson, 1988)

The French Chateau: Life · Style · Tradition
by Jean-Bernard Naudin and Christiane de
Nicolay-Mazery (Thames & Hudson, 2000)

Provence — Art, Architecture, Landscape
by Christian Freigang and Rolf Toman
(Könemann, 2000)

Style Elle Deco by Jean Demachy and François Baudot (Filipacchi, 2001)

Elle Decor: The Grand Book of French Style by Jean Demachy and François Baudot (Bullfinch Press, 2001)

Paris Interiors by Lisa Lovatt-Smith (Taschen, 2004)

Private Houses of Paris: The 'Hôtel Particuliers' Revealed by Jean-Bernard Naudin and Christiane de Nicolay-Mazery (Tauris Park Books, 2000)

Paris Hotel Stories by François Simon and Daniel Aron (Assouline, 2003)

Jacques Garcia: Decorating in the French Style by Franck Ferrand (Flammarion, 1999)

Alberto Pinto Classics by Phillipe Renaud (Rizzoli, 2001)

Jean-Michel Frank by Léopold Diego Sanchez and John D. Edwards (Editions du Regard, 1997)

Jean-Charles Moreux: Architecte— Décorateur—Paysagiste by Susan Day (Norma Editions, 1999)

A House is not a Home by Bruce Weber (Bulfinch Press, 1996)

Gardens of the French Riviera by Louisa Jones and Vincent Motte (Flammarion, 2002)

Gardens in Provence by Louisa Jones and Vincent Motte (Flammarion, 2002)

Mediterranean Gardens by Jean Mus, Dane McDowell and Vincent Motte (Flammarion, 2005)

French Country Hideaways: Vacationing at Private Châteaus & Manors in Rural France by Casey O'Brien Blondes (Rizzoli, 2005)

acknowledgements

Very special thanks are due to the many people who made invaluable contributions to the publication of *My French Life*: Julie Gibbs, Claire de Medici, Debra Billson; and especially Carla Coulson for her beautiful and vibrant photographs.

My sincerest appreciation to Hugues Bosc, Jennie Laplaisse and their team of craftsmen who brought Mas de Bérard back to life. To Michel Semini, thank you for your vision, creativity and expertise in the design and transformation of the garden.

Thank you to Madame Ducreaux and her sister, Didier Ludot and his manager Dominique Fallecker, Cafe Le Nemours, Ladurée, The Ritz Hotel Paris, Chez Paul and Moulin Rouge for their generosity.

To Valérie Lucien, Gérard and Christiane Matteoli and my friends who so patiently listened and helped, and to everyone who willingly gave their time to be photographed on the streets of Paris or in the villages of Provence and Les Arènes d'Arles — a warm thank you.

My heartfelt gratitude goes to David, Emily, Venetia and Paddy for their unfailing love, support and enthusiasm.